Thailand:
Development Planning in Turbulent Times

by

George Abonyi

and

Bunyaraks Ninsananda

* The ideas in this paper reflect the personal opinions of the authors (whose names are arranged in alphabetical order) and in no way represent the positions of their respective institutions.

University of Toronto - York University
Joint Centre for Asia Pacific Studies
Administrative Studies Building
York University
4700 Keele St.
North York
Ontario
M3J 1P3

ISBN 0-921309-89-9

Printed in Canada

Editing and design by Stephanie Gould and Caitlin Pollock

Cover design by Susan B. Hall, Instructional Media Services, University of Toronto

Acknowledgements

The authors wish to thank the two referees and Gilles Paquet for their many helpful comments; and Paul Evans and Richard Stubbs for their support in the publication of this paper.

Foreword

In recent years, Thailand's economy has grown so rapidly that it is now being widely talked of as the next Newly Industrialized Economy. In this volume of the *Asia Papers*, George Abonyi and Bunyaraks Ninsananda make a significant contribution to our understanding of how this rapid expansion of the Thai economy has been achieved. It will be of interest not only to those who have followed the developments in Thailand but also to the wider audience of administrators, development planners, and academics who seek a better understanding of development planning in developing countries.

This is the third volume in the Joint Centre's *Asia Papers* series. The series has been established to give those with an expertise in the Asia Pacific Region an opportunity to publish refereed papers which either on their own, or as a collection, fall between the length normally associated with a journal article and a book-length monograph. I would like to thank George Abonyi and Bunyaraks Ninsananda for their cooperation and Stephanie Gould and Caitlin Pollock for the editing, design and production of this volume.

Richard Stubbs
Associate Director

Table of Contents

Introduction

In the past three decades, Less Developed Country (LDC) governments have played an active role in *managing* the development process of their countries. This role included macroeconomic policies, investment in infrastructure, promoting and/or engaging in productive activities. Some form of development planning was generally part of this effort to manage the development process. A World Bank study notes that over 300 development plans were formulated in LDCs over this period.[1] Planning has differed widely among countries and has often changed over time in the same country. It has ranged from comprehensive central planning emphasizing central control and physical quantities, to indicative plans that use forecasts to guide investment decisions of independent decision makers in a competitive market environment.

Development planning as a coherent attempt to guide national development has an important role to play in the management of the development process. However, an increasingly complex and dynamic environment is placing new demands and constraints on the role and abilities of LDC governments to manage the development process. An increasingly *turbulent* environment may require changes in the role of planning, its technical and institutional base, and its relationship to the overall process of managing socio-economic development.

The purpose of this paper is to contribute to a general understanding of the requirements of planning development in a turbulent environment, focusing on the experience of Thailand. Our point of departure is the conviction that at this stage in Thailand's development, the planning process is faced with an increasingly complex task. This arises from changing internal conditions and demands, coupled with an increasingly turbulent external environment. The challenge to development planners is not only to generate appropriate policies and programs. More fundamentally, the challenge is to generate mechanisms and processes - a development planning system - that will anticipate, identify, and respond to key development issues in a changing environment.

In this paper, emphasis is given to form over substance in development planning, with an awareness that, ultimately, it is substantive decisions that influence the development process through specific interventions and resource commitments. However, we believe that substantive planning decisions are conditioned and constrained by the framework for generating such decisions. Coping with turbulence requires that the development planning system become even more sensitive to this relationship between form and substance. This puts increasing pressure on the planning system's scope, methodological and technical basis, and organizational and institutional framework in order to cope with growing turbulence.

Section two develops a framework to assist in interpreting the Thai experience. Section three presents a brief review of Thailand's experience with development planning from two perspectives. First, a summary of the development process over time. Second, a summary of the evolution of development planning: the changing focus and process of planning. We attempt to draw only the most general relationship between the two.[2] Section four identifies what we see as key characteristics of a planning system more likely to be responsive to an increasingly turbulent environment. The final section presents some concluding comments.

Some Background Concepts

The Concept of Development

The primary focus of development planning in practice, and as used in this paper, is on the economic, or more generally the socio-economic, subsystem. Within this context, a conventional way of establishing the relationship between planning and development focuses on the comparison of planned with actual economic growth. However, it is now generally accepted that development is not the same as, nor can it be reduced to, the concept of growth.

In general terms, we define growth as a lasting increase in size of some unit (e.g. per capita GNP).[3] Adding the qualifier *lasting* is intended to distinguish growth from random fluctuations. It implies that in the context of development, if growth is to *matter*, then growth or its effects must endure over some period of time.[4]

Although it is a useful concept, aggregate growth (such as per capita GNP) is both simplistic and vague. A socio-economy is a system, composed of elements in some relationship to each other: it has structure. Growth is likely to occur unevenly among these elements, and may lead to changes in both the elements and in their interrelationships. For example, growth is likely to occur at different rates and in different ways among different economic sectors such as industry and agriculture; among different industries within the industrial sector; among different geographic regions; among different socio-economic groups, and so on. These differential rates of growth have important implications for the overall structure of the socio-economy, and relate to the broader issue of structural change.

We define *evolution* as lasting changes in a socio-economic system that are linked, as distinct from a random succession of events and structures. For example, growth over time in industry's relative share of Gross Domestic Product (GDP) in relation to agriculture, implies an evolution of the socio-economy's structure including changes in the range of activities and their interdependence, associated organizational and infrastructure systems, decision making processes, and so on. Alternatively, these changes in the structure of the socio-economic system may occur without significant growth in particular elements. Evolution, then, encompasses growth in that it relates to change in both scale (e.g. size) and complexity (i.e. structure) over time.

Development may be defined as the evolution of human society, in response to its physical environment to bring about perceived improvements of the human condition.[5] Improvements are judged on the basis of closer approximation of the actual situation with widely accepted norms. These norms relate to perceived needs or issues such as unemployment (employment), poverty (income), and are likely to change as development evolves. Economic development is essentially a process of structural change, generally toward increasing complexity, characterized by an increasingly differentiated and integrated economic structure. It involves fundamental transformations in patterns of production, distribution, consumption, and in the physical and institutional frameworks for these activities.

The overall process of development transcends the technical and economic dimensions. It is also historical, political and cultural in nature. It is historical in that it is a process in time that covers long periods where the past conditions the future, but with many discontinuities. It is political in that it is an interactive process involving cooperation and conflict among different groups (stakeholders) with differing but interdependent interests.[6] It is cultural; basic values and institutions must be conserved, yet some cultural change is concomitant with development.

Development Planning

Conceptually, development may be thought of as two interlocking processes.[7] One of these we label, for lack of a better term, *real processes*, or those relating to goods and services, their production, consumption, distribution and exchange. This term does not indicate a *materialistic* viewpoint. It does not exclude a concern for quality of life, social justice, personal freedom or cultural values. For convenience, we label this dimension of development *real development.* We shall use the term *development* to mean these real processes and their outcomes.

The other type are *intellectual processes*, including information gathering, transmission, and processing; conflict resolution; decision preparation and decision making; and institutional design. Lumped together, we label these *management processes.* Development management in this context refers to the total set of processes guiding development by directly or indirectly affecting resource allocation and utilization.

In principle, development could be measured by a set of social and economic indicators that monitor real processes and their outcomes as changes in both scale (growth and decline) and complexity (change in structure). Conceptually, the role of development management is to move (or keep) key variables of the socio-economic system within acceptable limits, as reflected in the values of associated indicators such as per capita income, income distribution, poverty level, infant mortality, real exchange rate, and so on.[8]

The external environment also influences the development process: it *co-produces* development. Development is generally not only a function of domestic conditions, but also of external conditions and their impacts. These impacts vary according to the degree of an economy's openness, and the degree of complexity and change in the external environment.[9] In a relatively open economy, such as Thailand's, development depends in part on the development management system's capability to *manage the boundaries*; to anticipate, diagnose and respond to the changing external environment.

The institutional dimension of development management may take many forms. There is no *a priori* conflict between the concept of development management and the premise that a well-functioning market mechanism for allocating resources is a desirable institution, i.e. that micro-economic production and consumption decisions be left in private individual hands. Nor is it inconsistent with the premise that it is the *state's* (society's, community's) responsibility to assist in the provision of socially desirable goods and services that otherwise would not be produced to the desired extent. Development management's institutional dimension is then not simply the choice of *planning or markets* in particular settings. It involves the broader search for appropriate mechanisms and instruments - including *planning and markets* - to guide the process of development.

Development planning, as an element of development management, is an explicit and focused attempt to guide national development toward selected *desired futures.* It includes the identification and assessment of *alternative futures* and their translation into contemporary decisions. Operationally, planning involves the application of a range of technical and professional skills to the process of decision making with the purpose of anticipating and/or resolving particular (large-scale) problems or issues. Planning seeks to effect development through a direct impact on resource allocation, generally by guiding (constraining) program design and project selection intended to generate specified outcomes.

Conceptually, development planning may be differentiated from policy management, which is generally indirect and as a rule macro-economic and macro-social (as in monetary policy, fiscal policy, or trade policy). In practice, the boundary between policy management and planning is ill-defined: it is a function of choice of the form of the planning system. And, as will be seen in the Thai case, it is not unusual for development planning to include the formulation, implementation, and monitoring of policies, programs and projects which absorb resources and are intended to generate specified outcomes.

The development planning system has both form and substance. Form relates to characteristics such as scope, mechanisms, methodological and technical support, organizational and institutional framework. Substance relates to substantive decisions intended to influence the development process: the content of a development plan.

Both the substance and the form of planning can have a significant impact on development; the former directly, the latter indirectly. The impact of substantive decisions is easy to see; for example, in the specification of a public investment program. The indirect impact of choices in the form of planning are sometimes less apparent, but may be no less real. For example, these choices can range from a planning process which is restricted to the exclusive involvement of central government agencies, to broad participation by a wide range of interests. The scope can range from a comprehensive approach to planning that attempts to integrate policy management and project selection into the development planning framework, to a much more restricted one that limits planning to the preparation of the public investment program.

As development unfolds, changing demands and constraints are placed on both the substance and form of planning. For example, increasing industrialization, urbanization, and associated social and political changes are likely to generate different substantive concerns and guiding norms from those of a primarily rural and agricultural setting. Stated differently, the nature of the planning problem alters to a large extent as a consequence of a changing planning environment (both domestic and external). These changes may place new demands on the planning system, including its process, technology, and institutional framework.

The Nature of Development Planning Problems [10]

The nature of planning problems may be examined with the help of Figure 1. The horizontal axis shows the relative certainty of norms which guide the planning process;[11] these determine the suitability of a plan in terms of its responsiveness to perceived needs and its *acceptability* to relevant interests. The vertical axis shows the relative certainty of means-ends relationships (i.e. belief in the likely effectiveness of the means selected for responding to perceived needs).

In cells I and II, it is assumed that norms are known and agreed upon, and can be formulated as standards against which alternative courses of action and their outcomes are evaluated. In cells III and IV, norms are ambiguous, multiple and conflicting. It is difficult to assess the suitability and acceptability of activities with respect to guiding norms that are either ill-structured or changing.

On the horizontal axis, in cells I and III, it is assumed that *feasible* means-ends relationships are known.[12] There is a high level of certainty about expected contributions and impacts of planned programs and projects, with respect to perceived needs and associated norms. By contrast, in cells II and IV, means-ends relationships are ambiguous even when, as in cell II, norms are clearly defined. The contribution of planned activities to norms guiding problem resolution is uncertain.

The planning problems in cell I are *well-structured.* They are characterized by well defined norms and well understood means-ends relationships. The suitability, acceptability and feasibility of development plans can be clearly established. By contrast, problems in cell IV are *ill-structured* or *wicked.*[13] Here, explicit agreement on norms is lacking and means-ends relationships are not clearly understood. Movement away from the well-structured problems of cell I toward the wicked problems of cell IV involve increasing uncertainty.

Figure 1. The Nature of Development Planning Problems [14]

Norms / Means-ends relationships	Norms are well-defined	Norms are ambiguous or in conflict
Means-ends relationships are known at least probabilistically (i.e. well-defined)	I	III
Means-ends relationships are highly uncertain (i.e. ill-defined)	II	IV

In effect, all the problems outside cell I are ill-structured in that uncertainty is associated with the definition of means-ends relationships (cell II), norms (III) or both (cell IV).[15] For the purposes of this paper, we can collapse the two dimensions discussed above to a single scale. A well-structured problem corresponds to cell I, and an ill-structured problem corresponds to cells II-IV, keeping in mind that the source of uncertainty may differ among ill-structured problems. A key nature of uncertainty for planning problems relates to changes in the planning environment.

The Planning Environment: Stability and Turbulence

A socio-economic system is in some sense always in a process of transition. For example, the composition of products and processes in an economy is continually changing. The concept of stability then refers to periods of gradual, marginal and relatively smooth change. *Big* change is perceived in this context as a relatively smooth transition involving the accumulation of marginal shifts. In periods of stability, behaviour seems to follow understandable rules, resting on relatively well-defined, well-understood and shared premises. There are parameters that give regularity to behaviour and decisions. In economics these parameters may include market or more generally industry structure, key characteristics of the production process, technological developments. In politics, parameters may encompass the operations of critical institutions such as bureaucracies, institutional arrangements with respect to power distribution and decision making, the process for changing governments/leaders, the type and range of social groups and their relative power relationships. In the physical environment, parameters may broadly define the continued availability and accessibility of key resources. Taken together, these parameters define the *rules of the game*, providing a shared environment as the stable basis for decisions, plans, and expected outcomes.

In turbulent times, change can no longer be understood as the smooth accumulation of marginal shifts. Change involves fundamental discontinuities in structure and behaviour. In these times, the parameters that define the conditions for stability are themselves changing. For example, the pace, extent and impact of both product and process innovation may be accelerating, leading to fundamental changes in basic structure of key markets and industries; radically altering the competitive structure of industries (and nations); which may in turn lead to dramatic changes in the power relations of various social groups. In this setting, appropriate behaviours and associated outcomes, for example in economic activities, may be uncertain and unpredictable. The parameters themselves are inherently unstable: the rules of the game are in a state of flux.

Turbulence refers to an environment in which both the rate of change is increasing, and different types of changes are interconnected.[16] This increases the uncertainty and complexity facing planners and decision makers who must manage in these environments.

As in the earlier discussion of the planning problem (Figure 1), an increasingly turbulent environment may be characterized as one in which increasing uncertainty is likely to be associated with either the definition of norms guiding the planning process (cell II), the means-ends relationships implicit in planned activities (cell III), or both (cell IV). That is, the transition to turbulence is likely to involve a shift in the nature of the planning problem from predominantly well-structured to increasingly ill-structured.

Relationship Between the Planning Context and the Planning System

The relationship between the planning problem and the planning environment, and their joint implications for the planning system may be examined with the help of Figure 2. The vertical axis differentiates between well-structured and ill-structured problems. In cells I and III, the planning problem is assumed to be well-structured, with both norms and means-ends

Figure 2 Planning Context

Environment / Planning Problem	Stable	Turbulent
Well-structured	I. Selection	III. Control
Ill-structured	II. Search	IV. Adaptation

relationships assumed known and agreed upon. In cells II and IV, either the norms or the means-ends relationships, or both, are not known or agreed on with any degree of certainty.

The horizontal axis differentiates between stable and turbulent environments. In cells I and II the planning environment is assumed to be stable, characterized by gradual, marginal and relatively smooth change. In cells III and IV, the environment is assumed to be turbulent, with change involving fundamental discontinuities in structure and behaviour.

The planning context in cell I is characterized by certainty and stability. The norms which guide plan formulation and implementation are assumed to be clearly defined (or definable) and change only marginally over time. A set of feasible means consistent with these norms is also known, or may be defined, and remains valid over time. The focus of the planning system is on the *selection* of the most appropriate ends-means combination consistent with both norms and resource constraints. Efficiency considerations also dominate in plan implementation, given a known and relatively unchanging planning environment.

The planning context in cell II is also characterized by a stable environment, but here the planning problem is ill-structured. The planning system must focus on the *search* for acceptable norms to guide the planning process, and/or for feasible alternatives consistent with norms. If the search is successful, the ill-structured problem is transformed into a well-structured problem approximating cell I. However, if the uncertainty associated with norms and/or means is not significantly reduced, then the suitability, acceptability or feasibility of the plan remains uncertain and subject to dispute.

In cell III, the turbulent environment presents a new type of constraint. The salient characteristic of the planning system in this context is the *control* of plan implementation in a complex and changing environment. Having selected the most appropriate ends-means combination (as in cell I), the planning system must now focus on adjusting plan implementation to environmental disturbances to ensure outcomes consistent with expectations. This is likely to be a difficult task given the nature of turbulence. In fact, cell III is likely to be an unstable state. The well-structured planning problem may begin to unravel under the pressure of environmental change, shifting the planning context into cell IV. As a consequence, the development plan may no longer be suitable, acceptable or feasible. Attempts to maintain norms and ends-means relationships in this context that are no longer viable are likely to lead to unexpected and perhaps undesirable outcomes. A focus by the planning system on control in a planning context shifting from cell III to cell IV is likely to be at best ineffective, at worst, damaging to development.

The most complex planning context is cell IV. Ends and means, as well as environmental characteristics, are ambiguous and in a state of flux. An environment which changes in fundamental ways is likely to complicate the search for appropriate norms to guide the planning process and/or appropriate means consistent with those norms. In turn, ends-means relationships deemed appropriate at the time of plan formulation may lose their validity during implementation. To compensate, the planning system must focus on the continuous adjustment or *adaptation* of ends and means both to each other, and to a changing environment. The complexity of the planning task relates to plan formulation and plan implementation. Suitability, acceptability and feasibility of the plan cannot be taken for granted for any sustained period.

The infrastructure development requirements of Thailand's First and Second Plans (section 3) offer an example. They involved relatively well-defined norms, relatively certain ends-means relationships, and were planned and implemented in a stable environment. However, the Rural Poverty Alleviation Program of the Fifth Plan, or a focus on improving the external competitive position of the Thai economy (a key component of the Sixth Plan), impose very different requirements on the planning system. In both cases, it is much more difficult to define the desired outcomes and the strategies required to implement them in a complex and uncertain environment completely and unambiguously.

It is useful to summarize two prototypes in order to explore the implications of different contexts for the planning system. In addition to illustrating the more general issue, these two approaches have direct relevance to the Thai experience.

Two Approaches to Development Planning: Optimizing & Interactive

The particular characteristics of any given development planning system are likely to be better suited to deal with some types of planning contexts than others. The two prototypes summarized here, the *optimizing/centralized* approach and the *interactive/decentralized* approach, embody very different assumptions about the planning context in general, and about managing environmental change in particular.[17]

The *optimizing/centralized* approach involves defining and maintaining a well-specified strategic direction while coping with environmental disturbances that are perceived to be largely predictable and primarily transient. It assumes the planning environment, and the planning objectives and associated strategies in that environment are fundamentally stable. In this approach, the definition of norms and the selection of means are centrally determined, although a wide range of information sources may be utilized indirectly. Generally stated, it centralizes decision-information systems in order to support planning and the management of implementation by central institutions, usually at the macro level. The assumption is that the planning and implementation of decisions emanating from the centre can accurately reflect both changing conditions, and differing, and perhaps changing, perceptions and preferences of a wide range of interests with respect to both ends and means. The centre is assumed to be able to *optimize* development.

The *interactive/decentralized* approach proceeds from two basic assumptions. First, that both information and real power are dispersed. Second, that the planning context is complex and dynamic. As a consequence, those with a stake in - and with knowledge of - the perceived problem and proposed resolutions (stakeholders) must be linked directly to the planning and implementation process. The setting of norms, the selection of means and their adjustment over time are assumed to require direct inputs from relevant interests in order to generate viable and implementable plans. The centre then acts as coordinator and facilitator of an interactive planning process, in addition to providing overall guidance and technical support.

The two approaches may be projected against the different planning contexts, yielding Figure 3. The optimizing approach is likely to be most effective in a cell I environment of well-structured planning problems and stability. If ends can be defined, agreed upon, and remain stable over time, this approach provides a powerful framework for selecting the best (or optimal) ends-means combinations to address given problems. These are likely to remain valid over time in a stable environment, putting limited demands on the planning system to adjust. The centre can then manage the planning process, given prior and continuing agreement on ends and means.

A cell IV context, characterized by ill-structured planning problems in a turbulent environment, presents the other extreme. No centralized system is likely to be able to structure the planning problem with any sustained effectiveness. This includes the resolution of differences in perceptions and preferences among different groups and the management of an environment changing in fundamental ways. Guided interaction among different stakeholders is likely to be required for managing both the plan formulation and plan implementation process. The key roles of a central planning agency in this context are likely to relate to both technical analysis and process management, facilitating and coordinating an interactive planning process.

Figure 3 Planning Context and Planning Systems

Planning Problem \ Environment	Stable	Turbulent
Well-structured	Optimizing	Interactive/ Optimizing
Ill-structured	Optimizing/ Interactive	Interactive

Cells II and III present a mixed picture. Elements of both the optimizing and interactive approaches may be useful in both types of settings.

In cell II, the key task is to structure the planning problem. If the uncertainty relates to the definition of norms, the optimizing approach may be limited in its effectiveness. The planning system must also play an interactive role in mediating and reconciling conflicting interests. Similarly, for complex or new types of planning problems the search for suitable and acceptable means may require expanded interaction with relevant stakeholders. Elements of the interactive approach may then be coupled with the optimizing approach in the attempt to bring structure to the planning problem. If the planning problem can be relatively well-structured, the optimizing framework may be sufficient to manage implementation in a stable environment.

In cell III, elements of the optimizing approach may be used in both defining the structure of the planning problem (as in cell I), and in managing plan implementation in a changing environment. The predominant assumption relates to the continued validity of ends-means relationships in a turbulent environment. As noted above, this may be problematic. To enforce the implementation of plans in an environment where they are no longer viable is then likely to hinder the development process. Therefore, elements of the interactive approach may be used both to provide signals that norms and ends-means relationships defined earlier are no longer valid in a changed environment, and to assist in defining more appropriate ones.

The implication of the above is that if the planning context moves from cell I toward cell IV, the form of the planning system must also change if it is to remain effective in supporting the development process. In Thailand, the planning context has shifted over time out of cell I. This has created new conditions for the planning system, which has attempted to adjust in various ways. Now, on the threshold of the next (Seventh) plan, changes in the planning context seem to be even more pervasive, primarily the consequence of an increasingly turbulent environment that is also generating planning problems that are increasingly ill-structured (movement toward cell IV).

In the next section we will review briefly the evolution of both development and development planning in Thailand from 1961 to the present. The nature of the challenges facing development planners now and in the medium term will be discussed in the first part of Section 4. The second part of section 4 outlines what we perceive to be some of the characteristics and building blocks of a planning process necessary to respond to the challenges of turbulence, as reflected in the Thai experience.

Thailand's Development Planning Experience: 1961-1988

The past 27 years of development have pushed Thailand into the ranks of middle-income developing countries. Thailand has been able to sustain growth rates of around 7 percent per annum on average during the 1960s and 1970s. This high growth rate was accompanied by progress in poverty alleviation as demonstrated by the decrease in the proportion of the population under the poverty line, from about 57 percent in the early 1960s to 24 percent in 1981.[18] Careful management of the economy as well as the dynamic nature of the economic structure has successfully steered the Thai economy through changes in the international economic environment.

Thailand's performance in both economic growth and in poverty alleviation slipped in the early to mid-1980s largely due to a hostile international economic environment that affected all countries. However, in relative terms its growth rate still remained about 2 percent above the average for middle income countries, and Thailand continued to be highly respected abroad, as evidenced by its very favourable access to international credit markets.[19] In 1987, Thailand again experienced a high rate of growth of 8.4 percent, climbing to 11 percent in 1988. There is every indication of the potential for continued high growth rates into the 1990s. A high level of economic performance and stability are seen as providing the preconditions necessary for addressing key concerns such as continued poverty alleviation and employment generation. At the same time, an important focus of planners is on continued economic restructuring (e.g. diversification of product-market base of the economy) and producing flexible development management mechanisms in order to better respond to changing conditions and reduce the associated risks.

In supporting the development process, planning has historically been conservative in nature, and limited in scope. This conservative approach to public financial management and investment, and the continued reliance on the private sector, has been buttressed by the availability of physical resources, and by the religious and cultural traditions which encourage social cohesion.

The philosophical orientation of public sector activities has not changed fundamentally since the First Plan (1961-1966):

> "...in Thailand, increased output will be most readily secured through the spontaneous efforts of individual citizens, fostered and assisted by Government, rather than through the Government itself entering into the field of production."[20]

The First Plan went on to state that

> "...the key role of the public development program is, therefore, the encouragement of economic growth in the private sector and the resources of Government will be mainly directed to projects...in the...economy which have this objective in view."[21]

Although both the form and content of development planning have changed over the past 27 years - including expansion from solely economic to both economic and social planning - the basic philosophical orientation has remained consistent, and in fact is a central theme of the present (Sixth) Plan.

The increasing uncertainties in the changing international economic environment, and the evolving nature of domestic development raise ever-new concerns as the decade winds down. New challenges are posed to Thai planners. The general framework, institutional structure, and technical base of planning must all adjust to the challenges of development planning in a turbulent environment.

Growth with Stability: The First and Second Plans

Infrastructure-Led Growth: The First Plan

Development planning in Thailand began as a response to a failure in the development management system: the failure of the public resource allocation process (the budgetary system) to address the more fundamental needs of the economy. Pre-eminent among perceived needs was the provision of basic infrastructure. The inability to incorporate large infrastructure projects into the budgetary process was due primarily to the absence of a multi-year planning framework needed to accommodate large projects involving investment over several budget years. In 1959, as an institutional response to the problem, the Royal Thai Government (with the assistance of the World Bank) set up a central planning agency, the National Economic Development Board (NEDB). It bore the responsibility for preparing multi-year development plans. This later became the National Economic and Social Development Board (NESDB), reflecting the changing perception of development and development planning.

The First National Economic Development Plan was launched in 1961 to cover the six years between 1961-1966. This plan was primarily an aggregation of the perceived needs of various government agencies for infrastructure development. Thus the First Plan was essentially a multi-year financial allocation program for the public sector, involving primarily financial arrangements for the construction of selected basic infrastructure projects. This reflected the concept of an infrastructure-driven growth strategy as the basis for development. The fundamental assumption of the development plan was that rapid economic growth was the key to development, and that this could not take place without an adequate infrastructure network, including transportation and communication facilities, irrigation systems, public utilities such as power, and so on.

The provision of infrastructure was seen as the key to improving the investment climate necessary for capital accumulation, with a focus on import substitution industries. It was also seen to respond to perceived needs of the general, overwhelmingly rural population by facilitating the expansion of cultivable areas through new road networks and irrigation systems.

During the second phase of the First Plan (1964-1966), attempts were made to ensure consistency between the macro-policy framework and the investment program of the plan. A project-based approach to development planning was initiated through early developments in the systematization of the management of the project cycle, following the World Bank. Nevertheless, the First Plan was primarily a financial allocation plan focusing on infrastructure development. Its preparation was essentially the work of the central government, in particular NESDB and the various ministries, with little participation by non-governmental interests.

Growth with Distribution: The Second Plan

The Second National Economic and Social Development Plan was implemented in 1967 to cover the period 1967-1971. Although the main strategy of the Second Plan continued to focus on infrastructure-led growth, it was more comprehensive in design than the First.

The Second Plan integrated local governments and state enterprise into the public sector investment program. As the new name implies, the scope of development planning was expanded to include social issues, incorporating social development (e.g. education), along with economic activities.

The Second Plan also touched on the role of the private sector in development in the particular contexts of industry, trade and services. Selected policy measures were aimed at the development of the industrial and commercial sectors. These included - following the establishment of the Board of Investment during the First Plan - the enactment of several industrial promotion acts to provide incentives for investment, including foreign investment in manufacturing activities. Policy measures were also intended to promote the banking system in order to provide a financial base for trade and production.

Improvements in the planning system concentrated on further improvements in *optimizing* the management of the project cycle, partly by importing more World Bank technology. The optimization of public investment decisions was extended from project planning to regional development through the introduction of spatial planning.

The process of planning also changed, expanding in a restricted way participation in Plan formulation. For the first time, committees representing the range of relevant public sector agencies were established and were responsible for developing sectoral strategies.

The Second Plan then enlarged its coverage on a more integrated basis, expanding the concept of development implicit in development planning. However, it still focused analysis at a highly aggregate level and treated non-government interests such as the private sector, the main engine of growth, as a residual. This was also reflected in the somewhat wider, but still very much restricted participation in the planning process.

Development during the First and Second Plans

The period of the First and Second National Economic Development Plans (1961-1972) was one of rapid growth and stability. The average annual growth rate of about 8 percent far exceeded the average annual growth rate of 5 percent in the 1950s. At the same time, inflation was kept at an average annual rate of 2 percent. This development was a function of both world economic conditions, and the ability of the Thai economy to respond.

The international economy in the period 1961-1972 was relatively stable and predictable. Changes were both relatively orderly and beneficial to Thailand's development; world trade expanded rapidly, primarily between developed countries, but also providing fast-growing markets for raw materials and food exports from LDCs. In addition, the transition in many developed countries toward higher levels of technology led to a transfer of more labour-intensive and light industries to LDCs. This was accompanied by large inflows of capital in the form of aid and loans. The expanded American role in the war in Vietnam during the Second Plan contributed as well to a high level of investment (i.e. American military expenditure) in Thailand, helping to stimulate the economy. Other foreign investment, however, began to decline, especially in the second half of the Plan. Thailand simultaneously experienced declining world markets for two of its key commodity exports, rice and rubber. Nevertheless the overall effect during this period was a favourable external environment to Thailand's development.

Development, as measured by selected (economic) indicators reflecting the particular focus of development planning, was judged to be a success during both plans. In general terms, the expansion of agriculture and domestic demand were the key elements of growth during this period, accompanied by stability (e.g. of prices) and balanced growth among sectors. In particular, extensive basic infrastructure was put in place during the First Plan, leading to the expansion of agricultural production and stimulating investment in both import-substitution industries and resource development. The agriculture sector grew at an average rate of 6.45 percent per annum. Industrial expansion averaged 12.2 percent per annum, including an annual growth of 15.3 percent in mining and 11.3 percent in manufacturing, involving primarily import-substitution activities.[22] A favourable external environment also supported the expansion of exports at an annual rate of 8.6 percent, further opening the Thai economy to the international environment. The investment and economic expansion during the First Plan period was financed mainly by domestic savings, averaging 26 percent of GDP per annum, as compared with an annual average investment level of 25.4 percent of GDP. In addition to the high rate of growth, development during the First Plan was accompanied by stability, both external and domestic, as evidenced by a current account surplus of 0.6 percent of GDP and an inflation rate of only 2.3 percent per annum during the period.

The Second Plan was similarly successful, as shown by economic indicators. The production structure of the Thai economy began to diversify and the economy grew at an annual rate of 7.2 percent, with a low inflation rate of 1.5 percent. The ratio of exports to GDP stood at the end of the Plan at 17.4 percent. However, for the first time the increase in investment exceeded the increase in savings, with savings averaging 20.4 percent of GDP per annum, as compared with an investment to GDP ratio of 22.97 percent. The Thai economy began to draw on foreign savings for growth.

Growth was accompanied by structural changes in the Thai economy during the period of these two plans. The product-market base of the economy began to change in important ways. Within the agricultural sector, the provision of infrastructure, in particular an improved road network, led to the expansion of cultivated areas. This led to an increase in agricultural output because of expanded land rather than any gains from increased production efficiency. By the end of the period, agricultural output had diversified away from the traditional product mix dominated by rice, timber and rubber, to new crops such as maize, kenaf and tapioca. This diversification and increased output was due to a large extent to favourable export markets.

Diversification of agriculture was part of a broader transformation of Thailand's economic base. Agricultural output, although increasing in real terms, declined in relative importance from 39.4 percent of GDP at the beginning of the First Plan, to 26.85 percent by the end of the Second Plan. At the same time, the share of industry increased from 18.8 percent to 26.15 percent of GDP, with manufacturing output increasing from 12.4 percent to 16.9 percent of GDP. Within the manufacturing sector, there was a shift away from traditional processing activities to modern import-substitution activities, and more modestly, toward the development of an export-oriented industry. The share of services increased from 41.6 percent to 47 percent over this period.

The Thai economy increased its degree of openness. Exports and imports together increased from about 33 percent to over 40 percent of the GDP by 1972. The export structure diversified from traditional exports of rice, rubber, tin and teak to others such as fishery products, some manufactured goods, like textile, and new export-oriented agricultural crops. The composition of imports shifted toward an increased share for capital goods, raw materials and semi-finished goods to support import-substitution industries. As a consequence, there was limited linkage between growing industrial production and the agricultural sector. The pattern of production led to a growing dependence on imported technology and inputs (including capital), and to limited employment generation from the expansion of manufacturing activities.

The benefits of development were relatively well distributed during this period. Although the focus of development planning was on economic growth, significant gains were made in poverty alleviation; they were, however, mostly the secondary result of a growth-oriented strategy. The incidence of poverty was reduced from approximately 57 percent in 1962 to about 39 percent in 1969 largely owing to the expansion of agricultural production.[23] Since most agricultural production in Thailand is by small-holders, the income growth in agriculture accrued primarily to the rural producers. However, poverty remained a significant concern, and one that was unevenly distributed throughout the country. Although significant absolute gains were made in income growth for the majority of the population, the income gap among various groups and regions widened. The most significant gap was the rapidly increasing disparity between the Bangkok-centred region, where much of the economic growth was concentrated, and the rest of the country.

In summary, development during the period of the First and Second Plans was consistent with the aim of development planning. Infrastructure-led growth resulted in high aggregate growth rates, diversification in economic structure, and significant aggregate gains in poverty alleviation. However, the context of planning changed as the Third Plan approached. There was specifically a perception that the nature of the growth resulted in increasing inequalities among both groups and regions, and that this had to become a priority of development planning.

Broadening Development Planning: The Third and Fourth Plans

Toward Growth with Stability: The Third Plan

The Third National Economic and Social Development Plan was launched in 1972 for the years 1972-1976. The focus of the Plan was on maintaining stability. There was again some expansion of the scope of development planning to include new dimensions such as family planning and planning related to the role of the private sector in development. It also touched on the "national preparedness" issue, the integration of national security into overall development in an increasingly unstable external environment.

The Third Plan years saw a domestic environment of rapid political change, including increasing labour unrest and frequent changes in government, at least in part the consequence of the Indochinese conflict. At the same time, a changing external environment placed constraints on the relatively open Thai economy: the decline in value of the U.S. dollar, for example, followed by the first energy crisis, resulted in widespread stagflation in the world economy.

In this context, the primary concern of the Third Plan was to preserve economic stability in face of externally induced pressures on the economy, and of domestic political instability. Growth was to be maintained to the extent possible in a time of economic recession and stagnating investment, and in an environment of rapid political change. In addition, the pattern of growth was adjusted in order to respond to increasing political and social concerns, including a focus on reducing income gaps and other inequalities.

In general, the planning environment from 1972-1976 shifted toward an atmosphere of *crisis management.* The primary focus of development planning and management moved away from long-term planning and economic management, involving the optimization of public investment, toward coping with (largely externally induced) short-term fluctuations. No effective mechanisms, however, evolved to support a development planning and management system appropriate to cope with extensive short term fluctuations and instability in the context of long-term adjustment. In the process, the systematic project-based planning procedure imported from the World Bank eroded under an atmosphere of economic and political instability.

Public Sector Led Growth: The Fourth Plan

The Fourth National Economic and Social Development Plan was launched in 1977, covering the period 1977-1981. The focus of this Plan was on the adjustment of the economy after the first energy crisis, coupled with the further extension of the scope of development planning to the new areas of science and technology, natural resources and the environment. The Fourth Plan's emphasis included growth through increased public investment, and reduction of the income gap between rural and urban areas. Also, it emphasized the relationship between resource endowment and development, particularly in the agricultural sector, where the increasing scarcity of arable land led to an emphasis on increasing productivity on existing land.

The Fourth Plan introduced fundamental revisions in both the philosophy and mechanisms of development planning as a response to the unstable environment of the Third Plan. This involved taking the first steps toward a more interactive/decentralized planning process, as distinct from the optimizing/centralized approaches of earlier plans. Changes in the form of planning were deemed necessary by the NESDB in order to respond to both the economic crisis and political instability. Operationally, this shift involved three key changes in the planning system. First, the basis of development planning shifted from projects to issues. The intent was to define the key issues or problems requiring resolution, as the basic building blocks of the plan. In principle, a wide range of specific projects could then be generated as appropriate responses, depending on specific conditions and preferences. In other words, to cope with rapid changes in political decision making, the Fourth Plan was formulated as an issue-oriented indicative plan, under which a new government could allocate priority according to its own policy focus. Thus, the Plan would provide a framework for flexible response in a potentially uncertain political environment, such as the seven Cabinets of the Third Plan. The overall intention, then, was to construct a framework for development planning decisions that would remain useful through changing conditions and priorities. In effect, this issue-based approach incorporated the first steps in a continuing transition from project- to program-based management of development planning. [24]

As a second modification, the process of plan formulation shifted from a centralized, *top-down* approach involving primarily central government agencies, to one more participatory and interactive in nature. In this it reflected the changing political and social structure of Thailand. The formulation of the Fourth Plan involved participants from key sectors and professions, leading to the identification of the central development issues as perceived by the various groups making up Thai society. This broad participation was largely responsible for expanding the scope of the Plan, including such concerns as natural resources and the environment, science and technology, joint investment between the public and private sectors, distribution of social services, the role of women and children, and so on.

Thirdly, as an important step toward decentralization in planning, implementing agencies played a direct role in plan formulation. Responsibility for project initiation began to shift from the central agencies (e.g. the planning board), to implementing agencies, which identified areas for project focus within the Plan. However, project initiation and financial allocation were separated in the planning process; that is, the plan suggested project areas, but provided no associated allocation of financial resources.

In summary, the Fourth Plan began to introduce elements of an approach to development planning that may be characterized as *interactive planning*, distinct from the *optimizing* approach dominant throughout the first three plans. This may be seen as a response to the changing environment, characterized by ever-increasing economic and political instability, and complexity.

Development During the Third and Fourth Plans

Development during the First and Second Plan was judged successful in terms of economic growth. However, the nature of the growth, (i.e. its structural composition), was perceived to have resulted in growing inequalities among both groups and regions. Consequently, in formulating the Third and Fourth Plans, emphasis was given not only to continued economic growth and stability, but also to the problems of income inequalities, and inequities in the distribution of social services.

Thailand's economic growth averaged around 6.5 percent during the Third Plan, and 7.35 percent during the Fourth Plan. This aggregate growth was based on the continuing, rapid expansion of all three sectors; agriculture averaged a growth rate of 4.1 percent per year, industry 8.5 percent and services 7.3 percent, during the combined period of the Third and Fourth Plans.[25] The structural transformation of the Thai economy continued during this period. Agriculture declined to 20.44 percent of GDP, while industry increased to 30.65 percent and services to 48.9 percent of GDP by 1981.[26]

The benefits of growth continued to be relatively well distributed; the incidence of poverty declined to 32 percent in 1975, and to 24 percent by

1981.[27] Poverty was concentrated primarily in the Northeast and in parts of the North, where the fertility of the land is low, seeming to take on a more *structural* character. In line with the reduction in poverty, life expectancy and infant mortality rates improved significantly.

Development planners during the Third and Fourth Plan period were faced with increasing domestic and international change. Domestically, as noted, the Third Plan period involved labour unrest and frequent changes in government. Externally, the world economy in the 1970s was characterized by instability, two devaluations of the US dollar, sharp increases in the prices of commodities, and the quadrupling of crude oil prices. These instabilities resulted in inflation and recession in the developed nations leading to a decrease in world trade and a high level of unemployment in those countries.

The domestic and the external changes had a significant impact on both development and development planning in Thailand. The Thai economy opened more during this period with respect to the external environment. The proportion of international trade to GDP rose from 40 percent in the early 1970s to over 50 percent by 1981.[28] In particular, the share of imports in the GDP which had fluctuated between 19 percent and 22 percent in the 1960s, rose to 30 percent in 1980, with a significantly higher share going to oil. Exports increased from an approximate average of about 18 percent of GDP during the 1960s, to 20.2 percent in 1976, and to around 24 percent by 1981 with a reduced role for rice, the traditional principal commodity export.[29]

This increased openness enabled Thailand to benefit from the favourable conditions prevailing in the early 1970s. For example, during the Third Plan, the average annual increase in export earnings reached 31.48 percent as a consequence of high commodity prices. This led to a general growth of exports and to a diversification of manufactured exports. However, the added openness also made Thailand more vulnerable to changing world economic conditions in the more difficult period of the mid-and late 1970s. Sharp increases in the price of imports and exports, consequently, led to rising inflation, while at the same time the world economic recession weakened demand for Thai exports. What resulted was a stagnation of domestic investment, and increasing unemployment. In general, it became more difficult to insulate domestic prices and incomes from fluctuations due to changes in external conditions.

Thailand was able to absorb the impacts of the 1973/74 oil price increases and ensuing international economic upheaval with no significant slowing of growth. This was, in part, due to high commodity (export) prices, and to transfer and service account earnings. Greater domestic inflation reached the two digit level during the Third Plan primarily as the combined result of the energy crisis and price increases of other commodities. It was, however, brought quickly under control by a tight fiscal policy which was in part a by-product of higher trade values and lower real public expenditure growth. As a result, Thailand's domestic and external balance was restored by the mid-1970s. The current account deficit was kept at a manageable level of -2.7 percent of GDP, with the ratio of savings to GDP averaging 22.2 percent per annum, as compared with the ratio of investment to GDP of 24.9 percent.

By 1975, the primary focus was on the restoration of high growth rates, and the expansion of public investment and social service expenditure. The Fourth Plan accommodated a wide range of concerns, integrated into the Plan through the broad participation in plan formulation. This included concern with income inequalities and with inequities in the distribution of social services, leading to continuing pressure for investment, with limited guidance for trade-offs. The result was high and relatively unconstrained investment policies by both the public and private sectors, and an era of *overspending*. Contributing to the overspending was the failure of the public sector to adjust the tariffs of state enterprises, key agencies in the provision of public services, in line with the rising costs of production, particularly those of energy. As a consequence, the government had to borrow heavily to subsidize various state enterprises. These developments left Thailand in a vulnerable position when the second oil shock hit in 1979.

During the period of the Fourth Plan, the gap between savings and investment widened substantially. The ratio of savings to GDP stood at 18.9 percent in 1981, as compared to an investment level of 26.3 percent of GDP. This large savings-investment gap was reflected in the high current account deficit of -7.4 percent of GDP in 1981, with the public deficit in excess of 6 percent of GDP. The pressure of changes in the world economic environment, in particular the rapid increase in the price of oil combined with domestic *overspending*, to produce a continuing high annual inflation rate of 11.6 percent during the Fourth Plan period.

Although development was partially consistent with the focus of development planning during the period of the Third and Fourth Plans, there were also significant departures. These differences were in part due to more unstable and complex domestic and external environments (e.g. slow down of world economic growth); to emerging development issues (e.g. deterioration of natural resources); and to continuing unresolved concerns (e.g. poverty alleviation). All of these defined the context for the next development plan.

Adapting to Changing Conditions: The Fifth and Sixth Plans

Growth with Structural Adjustment: The Fifth Plan

The Fifth National Economic and Social Development Plan was implemented in 1982 to cover the five years 1982-1986. Given the experience of the Fourth Plan period, the Fifth Plan began with the assumption that high growth alone was insufficient to respond to growing domestic structural imbalances, and to severe external financial and economic constraints. The main themes of the Fifth Plan were to restructure the economy to enable future growth; and to restore financial stability and maintain credit worthiness in the international financial markets while retaining an acceptable growth rate.

The Fifth Plan was formulated in an environment of continuing instability of external economic conditions. As a response, the Fifth Plan placed specific emphasis on improving the efficiency and effectiveness of the development planning and management system. This involved two key dimensions. One dimension emphasized macro stability, not only through substantive measures such as tight fiscal policy, but also through the restructuring and/or creation of macro structures designed to improve macroeconomic management. The second dimension involved further adjustments of the planning system in response to a changing environment.

As part of the emphasis on macro stability through the improvement of the structural basis of central economic management, the National Debt Policy Committee (NDPC) was restructured and strengthened, and the Joint Public-Private Consultative Committee (JPPCC) was created. In the face of international financial instability and a growing foreign debt problem, the role of the NDPC was (and is) to help provide more timely responses to the changing conditions relating to foreign debt at both the macro policy and project review level. The JPPCC, composed of the top economic decision makers from both the public sector, and an increasingly diversified private sector, has the role of facilitating increased coordination of economic decision making between the two sectors.

Changes in the planning system involved modifications of the Plan formulation and management process, and of the structure of the Plan. The process of Plan formulation followed the participatory approach introduced in the Fourth Plan. It also incorporated the lessons of the resultant pressures of over investment, as occurred during the Fourth Plan period. Thus although a wide range of issues, concerns and priorities were generated through the process of participation by a broad range of interests, these were then *filtered* and incorporated into the Plan with consideration of existing resource (e.g. financial) constraints. Therefore the Fifth Plan reflected not only a process of broad participation, but also central choices as to relative national priorities.

With respect to Plan management, there was increasing awareness that in an uncertain environment the outcome of Plans was likely to be equally uncertain. As a response, the monitoring of Plan implementation was introduced in the very restricted form of a mid-plan review, focusing primarily on macro economic indicators and on the Eastern Seaboard Development Program.

Changes in the structure of the Plan involved the introduction of a program-based approach to development planning which reflected a continuing shift away from the project-based approach. This was a response to emerging development issues seen as transcending single sectors and implementing agencies, and requiring a broader, more coordinated and integrated response. The two issues selected for program focus were rural poverty, leading to the formulation of the Rural Poverty Alleviation Program; and basic industry development and associated geographic decentralization based on the discovery of energy resources on the East coast, leading to the formulation of the Eastern Seaboard Development Program. These two programs, in addition to providing the first examples of the program-based approach, also embodied two very different approaches to development planning. The Eastern Seaboard Development Program corresponded to the optimizing approach, and the Rural Poverty Alleviation Program, to the interactive approach.[30]

The Fifth Plan was launched during a period of depressed world economic conditions, but with the expectation of an improved economic climate in the near future (i.e. during the Plan period). The situation facing planners, however, worsened in the early phase of the Plan when the world economy did not recover as anticipated. Mindful of the experience of the Fourth Plan, the Royal Thai Government responded by implementing strict fiscal austerity measures, while developing measures, including refinancing and currency swaps, to smooth out the debt profile.

The primacy of restoring financial stability through austerity policy resulted in the delay of a number of capital-intensive projects. In particular, although some of the projects of the Eastern Seaboard Development Program were completed as planned, others were postponed. Other less capital intensive projects, including the Rural Poverty Alleviation Program, were judged to have progressed at a satisfactory rate.

External constraints on development during the Fifth Plan included an unexpectedly severe slow-down in world economic growth and international trade, increasing trade barriers, high real interest rates, and falling commodity prices. Economic growth averaged 5.3 percent per year, with most of the growth due to an expanding domestic market. This also increased the trade deficit through an expansion of imports, averaging 5.8 percent per annum. Inflation, however, was reduced to only 2.7 percent per year, on average, well below the near 11 percent rate of the Fourth Plan period.

Despite rapid response to fiscal instability, the public deficit grew during the Fifth Plan, though slowing in the second half of the period. This growth was largely the result of a failure to increase tax revenues sufficiently and to contain public expenditures to the planned extent. This aggravated the trade and current account deficits, both of which were higher than anticipated.

The labour force increased during the period of the Fifth Plan, at an average rate of 3.0 percent per year, including a sharp increase in the proportion of educated labour force. Given the slower than anticipated economic growth, employment generation increased at a rate of 2.2 percent annually, leading to a sharp increase in open unemployment.

In real terms, the structural development of the socio-economy continued. Over two thirds of public investment, and over half of total foreign debt was used to finance continuing expansion of infrastructure. Substantial gains were made in a number of areas; in energy production and the provision of pubic utilities, especially water supplies, and in social development, including population planning services, education, and public health systems.

Aided by the drop in oil prices and the realignment of major currencies, the restructuring efforts of the Royal Thai Government strengthened the nation's financial position so that the current account balance stood at 0.6 percent of GDP by 1986. Furthermore, the restructuring process involved not only the public sector, but also the private sector, which exhibited the same *overspending syndrome* during the Fourth Plan. Firms struggled to revitalize their operations through a major overhaul of their debt-equity profiles. This was coupled with the more careful screening of new borrowing by commercial banks, leading to large excess liquidity in the commercial banking system.

The public sector, was, to a large extent, able to manage the external debt crisis, and to significantly restore liquidity in the state enterprise system. The private sector reduced debt-ridden and inefficient activities, and began to *require* stricter financial discipline on new entrants through stricter control of debt-equity ratios on new credit extensions. In addition to restoring financial stability, the Fifth Plan still achieved a respectable growth rate of 5.3 percent, twice the average growth rate of the world economy. Gains in the reduction of poverty and inequalities, however, were more modest than expected, leaving these key issues the continuing concerns of development planners.

At the end of the Fifth Plan a number of issues focused the attention of Thai planners:

Macroeconomic Stability: Near the end of the Fifth Plan, the World Bank identified the central problem facing Thailand, as the need "to reduce the savings-investment gap, while continuing to grow".[31] The current account deficit was seen to be the result of low domestic savings, both public and private, as distinct from rising investment. The solution was perceived to involve stimulating domestic savings, while controlling foreign borrowing, and still maintaining an adequate investment level necessary to address central concerns of development such as employment and income generation.

Resource Limitations - Land Frontier and Poverty Alleviation: Thai agriculture has been very competitive on world markets because of low input costs per unit of yield. This has been due to a large extent to a land-extensive cropping system. A World Bank study attributes as much as 90 percent of the growth in agriculture over the last 20 years to the expansion of crop areas alone.[32] As noted earlier, this expansion has also played a critical role in poverty alleviation. However, farmers are now reaching the limits of readily accessible, good, arable land. This places increasing pressure on marginal lands and the declining forest cover. It also implies a greater need for intensification and mechanization in farming. It is also leading to decreases in productivity, employment and income generation in agriculture, particularly for poorer groups. It aggravates an increasingly seriously problem of resource depletion, putting potential constraints on future development.

Employment Generation: Approximately four million people who will require remunerative employment on a full-time basis are expected to join the labour force during the Sixth Plan period. Current trends in agriculture reduce the capacity for future on-farm employment. In addition, the changing mix of the labour force means an increasing proportion of educated youth coming on the labour market. Constraints on public expenditure limit the traditional job-generating role of the public sector, requiring that jobs for graduates be generated outside of government.

Improving the Development Management System: Although a specific emphasis of the Fifth Plan was improving the development management system, further improvements in both the efficiency and effectiveness of this system continued to be of concern at the end of the Plan period.[33] Included was the need to adjust the institutional framework, and the mechanisms and instruments of development management and planning in areas such as public investment planning, linking project design and selection to national development planning, coordinating public and private sector decisions; managing state enterprises, and so on. The need for on-going improvements in the development management system was, (and continues to be), the consequence of a Thai economy that is entering into a more complex and diversified phase, while exposed to a more competitive international environment in a time of increasing uncertainty.

Uncertainties in the World Economy: An important factor influencing Thailand's development, and development planning requirements, is the increasing complexity of the external (international) environment. This broad issue is introduced here as it relates to the Sixth Plan, and will be discussed in more detail in the section *Into the 1990s.* Two major dimensions of the issue generally involve growing uncertainty in key areas, such as the global financial system and market access, and increasing intensity and the changing nature of global competition. Given Thailand's open economy, these developments place important potential constraints on the Thai economy's capacity for employment and income generation. It also forces increasing emphasis in development planning on stabilization requirements and flexibility.

This has set the stage for the formulation and implementation of the current Sixth National Economic and Social Development Plan.

Growth under Uncertainties: The Sixth Plan

The Sixth National Economic and Social Development Plan, begun in 1986, covers the period 1986-1991. The key theme of this plan is to emphasize efficiency and improved quality in development activities, in order to improve the international competitiveness and self-reliance of the economy. It is intended to continue significant elements of the Fifth Plan, particularly, to maintain financial and economic stability, while accelerating the restructuring and diversification of the economic base.

In the Fifth Plan, the key role for growth and development was played by extensive public sector investment, involving both the central government and state enterprises. Successive years of revenue shortfalls, however, aggravated constraints on public expenditures. The Sixth Plan is intended to reflect the realities of public sector resource constraints, while providing a framework for responding to rapid, unpredictable fluctuations and constraints in changing international and domestic environments. The focus is to be on qualitative development as distinct from quantitative growth. That is, large-scale and capital intensive activities are to be kept at a minimum to support economic and financial stabilization. Part of this emphasis on qualitative development involves a continuation of the focus of the Fifth Plan on improving the development management system, now elevated to a central theme of the Sixth Plan. This includes widening its scope to areas such as *law and development* and state enterprise management, as well as sharpening and/or extending mechanisms introduced earlier such as program-based planning and participation in plan formulation.

An important theme of the Sixth Plan involves the reduction of the investment and production role of the public sector. This is intended to recognize the realities of public resource constraints, and to maintain flexibility and minimize risks in a dynamic and unpredictable external environment. The focus is on activities that do not involve major expenditures, but that could have a significant impact on economic performance and development: namely reform of the regulatory, legal and incentive frameworks; marginal extensions of, and limited improvements in, physical infrastructure; improving the efficiency of state enterprises. As the public sector, in effect, contracts its role in production and investment, growth for employment and income generation is to be led by a corresponding expansion of private sector activities. In this context, the public sector "will act primarily as coordinator, advisor and supporter of the private sector in various areas", instead of undertaking large capital expenditure itself.[34]

A major focus of the Sixth Plan is on diversifying the product-market base of the economy. This is intended to spread the risk burden both of individual producers, and the economy as a whole, through the diversification of income sources. This is especially significant in relation to the anticipated long-term decline in the role of the production and export of traditional agricultural goods. In particular, this diversification of the economic base is intended to build on local resources, while responding to expected changes in the international economy, such as market conditions.

The process of Plan formulation further refined the participatory process initiated in the Fourth Plan. It involved the comprehensive coverage of selected development issues through extensive participation of relevant interests, aiming at consensus in both the framing of development issues and of appropriate responses. The process also continued to sharpen the requirements for focusing attention on key development issues and their appropriate responses, and for trade-off among these issues in focusing resources. The intent was to both broaden the information base for planning, and to build public support for policies and programs.

The Sixth Plan continues the transition from project- to program-based planning, extending the programming approach to the Plan as a whole. In practice, the programs vary widely in terms of design, focus and coherence, and therefore in how easily they can be implemented. To respond to growing uncertainties in the external environment, flexibility is increased through the introduction of annual operational plans, increasing the opportunity for economic managers to adjust to changing external conditions. The operational plans are to be designed mainly by the implementing ministries in the specific context of each program, leading to improved planning capabilities at the ministry level. This reflects an attempt to decentralize the planning process to implementing ministries, and in the process, linking planning and implementation more closely.

Since the Sixth Plan is only in its third year of implementation, it is difficult to predict how development will evolve during the remaining period. However, improvements in the development management system implemented during the Fifth Plan, (e.g. management of foreign debt), have contributed to the successful restructuring and stability of the economy. This has allowed it to take advantage of the economic opportunities which began to present themselves during the first part of the Sixth Plan. These opportunities arose in part as a consequence of the realignment of currencies favourable to Thailand, of the successful expansion of Japan's domestic economy; and of the favourable intra-regional shifts in investment and production. As a result, 1987 and 1988 were very good years by most economic indicators. In particular, the economy grew by 8.4 percent and 11 percent respectively, spurred by an increase in foreign investment. Growth in manufacturing averaged 13.1 percent over the two years, with agriculture declining by 2 percent in 1987 under the pressure of low commodity prices, but rebounding to grow at 8.6 percent in 1988. The export surge continues at an accelerated pace, averaging 32.3 percent a year. However, Thailand's trade deficit has also increased, accelerated by the surge of foreign investment that has spurred imports of capital goods, and by increased imports of consumer goods, for a rise in total imports of goods averaging 42.9 percent per year. There is a feeling that with financial and economic stability well under control, there can now be increasing focus on addressing continuing development concerns, such as poverty alleviation and inequalities.

With optimistic projections for Thailand's economic performance in the 1990s, (e.g. IMF projections), there is at the same time concern for both emerging development issues, and for a continuing turbulent external environment. If Thailand is to continue its development process in the full sense of that concept, maintaining external stability while addressing key development issues, the development planning process must continue to anticipate and respond to changing conditions.

The Evolution of Development Planning

Since 1961, the domestic and external environments of development planning in Thailand since 1961 have been characterized by an evolution toward increasing complexity, involving both the growth and structural transformation of the socio-economy. Partly as a consequence, the development planning system has also evolved from a process of central allocative planning, restricted in scope, to a more interactive process focusing on a broader range of issues. In reviewing both the context of planning and the planning process, we could characterize the change as moving through three phases.

Phase 1. *Centrally Determined Public Investment Planning*

The planning context during the First and Second Plans, and into the Third Plan, can be characterized as relatively well-structured and stable. Both the domestic and external environment were relatively well understood by planners who could proceed on the basis of assumptions that were expected to remain reasonably valid during the planning period. Planning addressed the well-structured problems of infrastructure development and concentrated on optimizing public investment for economic growth. Development planning took the form of a top-down, direct allocative process by the central government that developed allocative criteria, and formulated allocative indicators. This process of centrally-determined planning to optimize public investment, was sufficient for the well-structured problems defining the restricted scope of planning activities, and the stable environment of the period of the First and Second Plans. However, by the Third Plan the planning context had changed, and the planning system was forced to respond in kind.

Phase 2. *Emergence of an Alternative Approach to Planning: The Interactive/Decentralized Approach*

The movement "beyond the stable state" began during the Third Plan.[35] Both the domestic and external environments began to lose their stability and predictability. A planning system focusing on centrally determined optimization of public investment for growth in a stable environment was no longer adequate. It now had to cope with a planning context characterized by externally induced short-term fluctuations in the economy, accompanied by domestic political instability. As a consequence, the development planning and management system attempted to respond in an ad hoc *crisis management* mode, but without developing effective institutional mechanisms for coping with extensive short-term fluctuations in the context of long-term adjustment.

The Fourth Plan implicitly accepted the fundamental transformation of the planning context and attempted to adjust the planning system in response. The intent was to create a framework that could accommodate change. The planning system was thus modified in important ways, including a shift from project- to issue-based planning, to extensive participation in plan formulation, and some decentralization of responsibility for project initiation to implementing agencies. This may be described as a shift to a more interactive approach to planning as a means for coping with a more unstable and complex environment.

The interactive process, however, was relatively unfocused and unconstrained. There was, for example, little guidance in the selection or prioritizing of key development issues or projects to guide the public investment program. Similarly, there was no emphasis on mechanisms for effectively translating such a plan into implementation requirements. This process of *unfocused participation* coupled with an increasingly unstable environment led to over investment and a growing debt problem by the end of the Fourth plan.

Phase 3. *Toward an Adaptive Planning Process: Competing Views*

The present phase of development planning in Thailand can be characterized as attempting to move in a more systematic way toward an *adaptive* planning system. The Fifth Plan focused explicitly on adjusting the development management system, including important modifications to the planning system, in order to cope with a changing environment. The process of broad participation in plan formulation continued, but was focused on selected issues - such as economic stabilization, rural poverty alleviation, and basic industry development - in a more comprehensive and integrated way. This led to the selective introduction of two programs in priority areas within the Plan as the basis for public investment. As noted, these two programs embodied very different approaches to development planning. In a further attempt to cope with the changing environment, the scope of the planning system was extended to the management of plan implementation through the introduction of a very limited mid-plan review.

The Sixth Plan further refined and extended adjustments in the planning system. The qualitative improvement of the development management system as a means for coping with the changing environment is both a central theme and a specific program in the Plan. The process of focused participation was further refined in the formulation of the Sixth Plan and applied to the definition of programs. Program-based planning was extended to the Plan as a whole, partly to increase coordination and integration in Plan implementation across sectors and agencies. Concern with implementation also takes the form of attempting to *decentralize* plan implementation through an emphasis on the role of non-central government *players*, including the private sector, Non-Governmental Organizations (NGO) and local government. The focus on linking planning and implementation is further reinforced through an emphasis on developing mechanisms for the monitoring and evaluation of plan implementation.

We can summarize the Thai experience with the help of Figure 4. The horizontal axis differentiates between planning systems that correspond more either to the optimizing or to the interactive prototypes. The vertical axis differentiates between stable and turbulent environments.[36] The six Thai development plans are then located in the matrix.

Development planning in Thailand has evolved considerably since the First Plan, and is likely to continue to adjust in response to a changing environment. However, key dimensions of a planning system appropriate to cope with increasing turbulence remain unclear. The following section summarizes the characteristics of the emerging *turbulent* environment that are likely to define the context of the next (Seventh) Plan.

Figure 4. Thailand's Development Plans

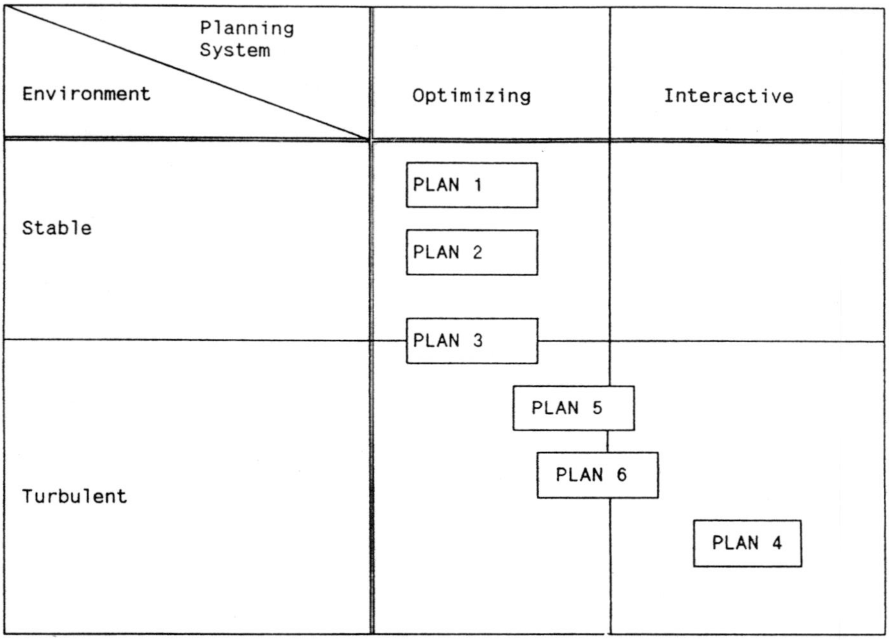

Development Planning in Turbulent Times: Into the 1990s

Transition to Turbulence

The Changing Domestic Environment

The domestic environment is expected to increase in complexity during the Sixth Plan. The issues noted earlier are expected to continue to be of concern beyond the horizon of the Sixth Plan, for example macroeconomic stability, employment generation, and increasing resource constraints. More generally, the structure of the economy is expected to continue to evolve in fundamental ways, presenting new issues to planners.

The present rapid growth of export-oriented manufacturing activities concentrated primarily in the central (Bangkok) region raises concerns about increasing economic dualism. There is concern about widening the existing income disparity between the industrial/urban and agricultural/rural groups. The present boom in commodity prices is seen as mitigating the effect only in the short term. It does not resolve the problem, especially in light of continuing protectionism in agricultural products on the world market. In addition, the economic disparities are likely to increase migration from rural to urban areas, creating problems of adjustment in both.

The high growth rate has resulted thus far in the expansion of economic activities, bumping up against existing physical (i.e. infrastructure) and human resource constraints. This poses two important concerns to planners. The first is the requirement to balance the extent and pace of a *second generation* expansion of physical infrastructure against the requirements of maintaining macroeconomic stability. The second issue relates to the problem of matching the skill structure of the labour force to a changing economic structure, as illustrated by the existing and growing shortage of technical manpower.

The required increase in the level of investment, especially if too rapid, is likely to widen the savings-investment gap, if the rate of savings cannot rise commensurately. To put the issue into perspective, the present rate of savings in Thailand is well below the NICs, at a time when many see Thailand in the process of evolving toward NIC status.

Thailand's recent economic performance has been fuelled by the expansion of exports. In this, the country's competitiveness is presently derived primarily from a competitive exchange rate and low wage rates, supported by effective macro economic management. With the rapid growth of the primarily urban industrial sector, wage rates are likely to rise along with a tightening labour market. This is also likely to be accompanied by more complex labour relations, in part as a response to the changing production structure, and to the changing composition of the labour force.

Another important factor in the present economic expansion is the rapid increase in foreign direct investment. This is likely to continue, with potentially significant implications for the structure and external links of economic activities.

Changes in the structure of the economy are being accompanied by changes in the political arena. New participants are emerging and power relations are changing; for example, different types of manufacturers, growing middle class, labour. These changes are expected to increase the differences in perceptions and preferences about key development issues and appropriate policies and programs. They are also likely to lead to changes in the institutional framework of the planning system.

The Changing International Environment

Given Thailand's open economy, the international environment is a critical factor in the country's development process. As an example of its importance, it is estimated by the World Bank that in 1981-2 Thailand effectively lost 10 percent of its national product due to external shocks.[37] An increasingly turbulent external environment, then, has important implications for Thailand's development, and for the development planning process.

The structure of the international economic environment is evolving in important ways. At the macro level, the key characteristic of the late 1980s and 1990s is likely to be the significant international adjustment necessary to correct the very large payments imbalances between the key currency country, the United States, and the other major industrial countries and some Asian NICs. The adjustment process is likely to effect the world trade and investment structure in general, and the structure and role of the Asian-Pacific economies in particular. Given the twin problems of a large external debt, accompanied by a large trade deficit, the American economy is likely to undergo significant readjustment in the medium-term. In consequence, it is probable that Japan and the NICs, the most dynamic exporting region of the world, will face declining exports to the United States, their major market. However, Japan, East, and South East Asia have the capacity to expand domestic demand faster than any other region. Therefore the expansion of intra-regional trade coupled with the presence of Japanese capital may lead to continued prosperity in the region in the long run, once the export readjustment stabilizes. This will most likely involve a realignment of production and export patterns among the countries of the region, with important implications for Thailand. In fact, there are strong indications that this process of adjustment is now under way.

Prior to 1985 Japan and the NICs concentrated on developing their own relations with the United States, with little emphasis on developing intra-regional trade. Exports to the United States drove all their growths. There has been a significant change since 1985, when the era of the cheap yen came to an end. Production bases have been relocated from Japan and the NICs (e.g. Taiwan) to other countries in the region (e.g. Thailand) in order to maintain international competitive position. For example, the regional distribution of Japanese overseas investment during 1985-1987 shows that the Asian share, primarily East and South East Asia, increased from 10.4 percent to 19 percent, and that the share to the United States declined from 46.8 percent to 36.2 percent. This development of horizontal division of labour among the countries of the region is accompanied by the expansion of domestic demand in these countries as a main engine of economic growth. This has led to a significant increase in intra-regional imports: Japan's imports from East/South East/South Asia increasing 31 percent from 1986 to 1987, as compared to an 11.8 percent increase in total imports from the rest of the world. In short, the outflow of investment and the opening of domestic markets in Japan and the NICs is resulting in a closer economic relationship among Japan, the NICs and ASEAN, changing economic conditions in important ways.

At the micro level, many industries are undergoing a process of global restructuring, primarily as a consequence of technological revolutions that reshape competition. These include developments in microelectronics and advanced new materials such as ceramics, information and communication systems, and numerically and computer controlled manufacturing processes. One element of this restructuring involves the declining importance of traditional sources of comparative advantage. New technologies are reducing direct labour costs to a smaller proportion of total costs in many industries; there is also an increasing globalization of markets for raw materials and other inputs, including capital. National capital markets, specifically, are merging into a global capital market that is characterized by large flows of funds between countries. This has amplified the volatility of exchange-rates with important implications for the flow of resources, goods, and investment.

At the same time, the international competitive environment is becoming more intense and complex. New players, primarily from East Asia, have emerged as important international competitors. Traditional players (primarily from the industrialized countries) experiencing decreasing opportunities in a slow growth environment at home, have made international competitiveness important at the level of both firms and governments. In attempts to protect domestic firms from intense international competitors, a new wave of protectionism is increasingly taking the form of various types of non-tariff barriers and trading blocks such as the European Community's unification, and the North American Free Trade zone.

Given the changes in the external environment and their domestic implications, coupled with the changing nature of development issues in Thailand, planners are faced with an increasingly turbulent planning environment. The challenge to development planners is then not only to generate appropriate policies and programs. More fundamentally, the challenge is to generate mechanisms and processes that will anticipate, identify, and respond to key development issues in the increasingly complex and uncertain environment.

Coping with Turbulence

An increasingly turbulent environment has important implications for the planning process. First, the potential for any single player, or "model", to fully understand the planning environment is low, necessitating multiple perspectives. Second, predicting the consequences of decisions and actions is increasingly difficult, requiring flexibility in the design of strategies, programs, and projects. Finally, the ability for any single player to control planned activities and outcomes becomes problematic. This requires, on the one hand, the increasing capability to monitor both the broad elements of plan implementation and its fit with a changing environment, and also the cooperation of various groups in the implementation process.

The planning system must, then, accommodate uncertainty and diversity in both plan formulation and implementation. Given that new issues and constraints are likely to emerge in the process of implementation, planning and implementation must be approached as interdependent activities that modify each other over time.

We can identify three broad requirements for an adaptive planning system that is likely to be more responsive to increasing turbulence in the Thai context: focused (managed) participation in plan formulation; guided (constrained) flexibility in implementation, especially in linking the macro plan to micro projects; and strategic monitoring of implementation. The role of each of these has been recognized to various extents in Thailand, but requires further development and better integration into the planning system.

Focused Participation: Interactive Planning

A key dimension of the growing turbulence of the planning environment in Thailand is a society/polity that is becoming increasingly heterogeneous with differentiated, yet interdependent interests with respect to the development process. There are growing pressures on the planning system to accommodate a broadening and evolving range of interests in plan formulation, program design and project selection.

At the same time, economic conditions are leading to a shift in the role of the public sector in Thailand from one of implementor (i.e. producer, investor) to one of facilitator and manager. Correspondingly, other groups are expected to increase their roles in implementing development. This requires that the planning system accommodate an increasing diversity of interests which must be coordinated and integrated in the process of plan implementation.

In general, the planning system is becoming increasingly drawn into explicitly managing the process of interaction with diverse stakeholders in both plan formulation and implementation.

In a turbulent environment with an increasing diversity of interests, some form of consultation with and participation by, relevant stakeholders is essential for the generation of implementable plans. This is necessary for two, interrelated reasons: first, because of information constraints on plan formulation; and second, management requirements of diffused control in plan implementation.

An increasingly turbulent environment places constraints on the information available to any single group, including technical experts such as planners, about the nature and implications of development issues and the characteristics of appropriate and implementable responses. Increased consultation and participation in the planning process then involves broadening the information base of plan and program formulation, and of project selection. That is, the formulation of implementable plans requires both the specialized knowledge of technical experts, and the substantive knowledge of stakeholders with particular perceptions, concerns and interests in the development process.

The process of consultation and participation in plan formulation is relevant not only in information acquisition. In a planning environment increasingly dependent on the actions of a growing number of diverse interests, cooperation by key stakeholders is necessary for plan implementation. That is, the implementation of any policy, program or project requires and assumes certain activities and attitudes by the stakeholders linked to the particular decision.[38] The process of consultation and participation is then likely to support implementation in two ways. First, it is likely to identify inappropriate assumptions implicit in policy or program or project design with respect to the preferences and potential behaviour of specific stakeholders. Second, consultation and participation is also aimed at building consensus. It is therefore likely to broaden the commitment of relevant interests to the development plan, and is more likely to ensure their requisite cooperation in plan implementation. Only mutually acceptable outcomes are likely to provide viable resolutions to shared problems.

However, participation in the planning process cannot be unconstrained: it must be focused and managed both procedurally and substantively in order to produce tangible outputs that respond to specific concerns. That is, the purpose of participation in development planning is to generate specific policy, program and project interventions that are responsive to specific problems. The role of the planning system is to facilitate, focus and manage the process. Thus, new demands are placed on planners and planning agencies as coordinators and managers of an interactive consultative process, in addition to their role as technical experts.

In Thailand, a number of steps have been taken to increase the consultative and participatory dimension of the planning process. At the macro level, the process of plan formulation especially during the Fifth and Sixth Plans has involved participation by key segments of society in both defining appropriate development issues, and in assessing appropriate responses. At the middle level, the creation of the Joint Public and Private Consultative Committee, and its extension to the provinces is intended to provide a mechanism for the explicit participation of private sector interests in the development management process. At the micro level, the Rural Poverty Alleviation Program of the Fifth Plan took primary steps toward participation by local, community interests in project selection. Although these developments are important, the challenge remains to further develop both the institutional and technical bases for managed consultation and participation in development planning as a means for coping with increasing turbulence.

Constrained Flexibility: Plans to Projects

The Role of Scenarios

A turbulent environment places a premium on flexibility in both plan formulation and implementation. Flexibility in plan formulation, the focus of this section, involves generating a plan that somehow accommodates alternative possible futures that could evolve from an environment characterized by increasing complexity, uncertainty and unpredictability. Flexibility in plan implementation, the focus of the following two sections, has two dimensions. First, it involves the simultaneous provision of focus and flexibility for resource utilization (e.g. project generation), leading to projects that are consistent with broad macro requirements and with *local*, micro conditions and needs. One approach to accommodating this involves the use of strategic programs as key structural elements of plans. The second dimension relates to the need to more closely link planning and implementation in a dynamic process of mutual adjustment. This involves monitoring broad elements of the plan and its environment as a basis for adjustment.

Flexibility in plan formulation requires an assessment of the likely performance of proposed strategies in alternative environments. Since there is no certainty as to the actual characteristics of the future environment, proposed strategies need to be assessed against different plausible *futures*, instead of developed from a single set of postulated events. The purpose is to formulate plans that remain viable (*stable*) in a range of alternate possible future environments, none of which can be predicted with any degree of certainty.

A useful technology for assessing the potential stability, or robustness of proposed plans involves the utilization of scenarios. Scenarios are representations of future states of a system, based upon assumptions about interactions among different trends and environmental conditions. They are useful to help identify and clarify major issues for discussion, and to provide a *screen* against which proposed strategies and programs may be projected. The scenario approach does not constitute a new method of forecasting: it provides a framework for utilizing data, forecasts and conjectures that may be generated by other techniques. Scenarios can effectively organize a variety of seemingly unrelated economic, technological, political, societal, and ecological information and translate it into a framework to support planning in a way that models, such as macroeconomic models, are not likely to do.

Scenarios deal with two worlds: the world of facts and the world of perceptions. Their aim is to gather, integrate and transform data, including forecasts and conjectures of strategic significance, into fresh perceptions.[39] To do this, scenarios structure the future into known and uncertain elements. The utility of scenarios lies in their exploration and expansion of known elements; events already in process whose consequences have yet to unfold; interdependencies among elements; breaks in trends; and conjectures about *plausible surprises*. Scenarios acknowledge uncertainty and aim at structuring and understanding it. They create alternative and internally consistent representations of possible future states. However, they are not quasi-forecasts, one of which may be right. They illuminate major forces driving the system, their interrelationships, and their critical uncertainties.

For example, there are a range of factors that are likely to affect the implementation of Thailand's external economic strategy, such as export development. These include economic factors such as commodity price movements, political factors such as protectionism in key markets, competitive factors such as likely strategies of key competitors, and so on; all of these could have a significant impact on Thailand's competitive position. Therefore, in developing the basis for an external economic strategy, it is important to somehow integrate and synthesize the important factors that will inevitably condition the success of such a strategy. Scenarios are powerful tools for this type of synthetic representation of possible futures.

Assuming an increasingly turbulent environment, it is difficult to confidently assert what shape the future will take. However, it is possible to identify alternative plausible futures that may emerge, utilizing current understanding of key factors, and incorporating different assumptions about their likely behaviour.[40] The use of multiple scenarios in plan formulation then forces planners to act on the basis that the future can never be exactly known, and that therefore viable plans must be able to accommodate a range of possible future environments. Plans supported by this approach are likely to be more flexible than those drawn up to meet a specific set of postulated events.

Another potential role of scenarios relates to the participatory and interactive dimension of the planning process. Scenarios can serve as a tool for communication among groups with different perspectives and interests. They can be used to elicit alternative perceptions and expectations about future environments and their implications for plan formulation and strategy development.

Developing scenarios of operational value is, at best, an uncertain art. However, there is an accumulated experience base both with the technology and the performance of scenario-based strategic planning, especially at the enterprise level.[41] This suggests that scenarios could be usefully integrated into the development planning process.

There have been limited attempts in Thailand to use scenarios to support plan formulation. This, however, has taken the restricted form of alternative economic forecasts generated by macroeconomic models. Given the experience cited above, the indications are that it may be possible to develop and apply a more general form of scenarios to support the plan formulation process.

<u>The Role of Strategic Programs</u>

The challenge in the transition from planning to implementation is one of being specific in areas of relative certainty, while providing both guidance and flexibility for implementation in areas of relative uncertainty. Strategic programs can play an important role in providing both focus and flexibility, and in linking planning and implementation. They can, in principle, provide a focus to broad development strategies, and a flexible framework for project development, coordination and integration.

A program-based approach to development planning differs both institutionally and conceptually from the traditional project-based approach. Institutionally, a project generally involves a single implementing agency (e.g. Department), which defines a particular and limited boundary for its activities and the issues which it addresses. A program generally involves multiple implementing agencies, and the needs of a program as a whole are likely to transcend the capabilities and mandate of any single agency. Any given implementing agency, such as a Department, has its own frame of reference, focus and needs, usually different from those of the program as a whole. Therefore, a key requirement in managing the implementation of program-based development is the coordination of the activities of individual agencies implementing the same program.

Conceptually, what makes a program out of the activities of individual organizations is some logical connectivity among these activities. This generally occurs when different projects, usually implemented by different agencies, contribute to a shared output (or respond to a common issue). The concept of a program involves defining the issue at a higher, policy level (e.g. sector, region, or complex issue), generally transcending the boundaries of a single implementing agency.

Operationally, a program can take many forms depending on the characteristics of the issue or area being addressed. In relatively well understood problems and environments, a program can be very specific in defining the nature of activities and investment required (e.g. projects). This may be the case in the development of physical infrastructure. With problems and environments that are only partially understood, a program may clearly identify some of the key *design criteria* for project development without being able to specify all the criteria necessary for project generation. This may be the case in a program relating to the diversification of agricultural production and markets. In still other cases where the problems and environments are understood only in general terms, a program may identify the broad dimensions of appropriate responses without being able to specify the particular requirements for project design. This may be the case in a program relating to the modification of formal and informal educational systems to provide skills for future economic activities that are known or anticipated only in very general terms.

Whatever their specific form, programs are a response to emerging development issues that transcend single sectors and implementing agencies and require a broader coordinated response. The characteristic that defines a program is some kind of coherence in or focus to the program as a whole, over and above individual projects and implementing agencies.

As discussed earlier, the concept of a strategic program was first introduced into development planning in Thailand during the Fifth Plan. Some of the difficulties in, as well as the benefits of program-based planning emerged out of that experience. Programs then became the structural basis of the present plan. In general terms, some of the programs of the Sixth Plan are grouped around issues such as the Program to Improve Management and the Role of the State in Development, and others around areas or sectors like the State Enterprise Development Program, Natural Resources and Environmental Development Program Rural Development Program. Structurally, programs are linked to strategies, which in turn support targets.[42]

In order to support flexibility in plan implementation, a new role of implementing agencies under the Sixth Plan is to develop operational plans for their particular areas of program responsibility. This decentralization is intended, in part, to transfer detailed program planning activities to those agencies with the best knowledge of specific conditions, and with the responsibility to make these plans work. This is intended to introduce flexibility into the system in that those closest to implementation determine required activities and therefore can adjust these activities as needed in order to assist in the implementation of broad program requirements.

In practice, the programs of the Sixth Plan vary widely in focus, coherence and design, and therefore implementability. The implications and requirements of the coordination and integration inherent in such programs place new demands on the development planning process. For example, the process of coordinating and integrating the annual operational plans of implementing agencies within a program framework is a new facet of managing plan implementation. More generally, although there is some previous experience, program-based planning on the scale implied in the Sixth Plan is a qualitatively new dimension of development planning in Thailand. This is likely to require adjustments in the technological, administrative and institutional dimensions of the planning system.

To illustrate the operational implications of program planning and management we focus on the general issue of levels of program management. Given that the requirements of each program are different, and that each is temporary (e.g. for the duration of the plan period), specific organizational demands of program management cannot be generalized. However, every program will require management at the strategic and operations level.

Operations management of program implementation involves managing in some form across line Departments (i.e. implementing agencies) from the perspective of the program as a whole. It implies managing, however loosely, program elements and activities, coordinating and integrating the activities of implementing agencies within the overall program context. Operations management activities may also require the provision of support activities to the program as a whole, such information systems support beyond those that exist in individual implementing agencies. Each operations management system must be developed separately for each program. However, administrative requirements and support systems may be generalizable to assist in program implementation.

Operations management of programs is inward looking, focusing on the activities and components of a program from the perspective of implementation. This is not the same as the issue of program viability, which focuses on the continuing validity of purpose and overall design. Program viability refers to the *fit* between the program and its environment, including the issues it is intended to resolve, and corresponds to what may be termed as strategic concerns in program planning and implementation. In the planning phase the emphasis is on defining the existing and projected need for the program; the type of program needed; and the general program configuration and objectives. In the implementation phase emphasis shifts to monitoring the continued viability of the program as a whole, including the implications of environmental changes for program purpose and structure.

Strategic and operations level management of programs, though linked, are fundamentally different in nature. They use different *conceptual languages* and frameworks; have different objectives; involve fundamentally different types of decisions with respect to different types of activities. As a consequence, it is important to keep the two levels of program management logically and organizationally distinct (though of course linked). Failing to make the logical separation of these levels can lead to situations where program management is assumed to be synonymous with operations management, since operational concerns are much more immediate and likely to monopolize attention. Program activities may then be implemented efficiently, yet the program as a whole risks being "out of phase" with emerging needs and changing conditions. It is not yet fully understood how requirements of program-based planning will be accommodated in the development planning system in Thailand.

Strategic Monitoring: Planning and Learning

A development plan by definition refers to the longer-term future of a country. Nobody - including planners and policy makers - know to what extent and at what points in time the plan will need to be modified as it is being implemented. However, it is inevitable that it must be modified to some extent for two interrelated reasons.[43] The actual environment within which the plan is implemented changes continuously, and the planners and policy makers have control of a relatively small part of this environment. It is therefore unlikely that any development plan will be implemented exactly as conceived, nor will it generate the expected outcomes precisely as prescribed. This is especially true in a turbulent environment.

Development planning, in practice, is to some extent a continuous process. It adapts contemporary decisions about the future to the evolving state of knowledge. Planning in some form is essential in order to address key development issues. However, the next most important feature of the planning process in a turbulent environment is the capability to modify the plan - to adapt implementation - on a continuing basis in light of new information on changing conditions.[44]

One can begin with a development plan that is expected to respond to selected issues and generate certain outcomes. However, in a turbulent environment, it must be treated as a broad working *hypothesis* about both the existing conditions and the requirements of the development process, as embodied in the plan. It becomes essential for the planning system to obtain information on a continuing basis on the progress and outcomes of plan implementation in order to be able to assess performance. Only then can the plan be adapted to changing circumstances and needs.

A key dimension of adaptive planning is, therefore, the monitoring of plan implementation, including monitoring the changing external environment as related to key elements of the plan. The broad purpose is to assess whether the direction, strategies and associated programs continue to be viable over time in light of changing conditions. The emphasis is on the general monitoring of plan implementation, as distinct from the detailed monitoring of individual program and project activities.

A strategic monitoring system is intended to provide information during plan implementation, with respect to direction setting and broad patterns of resource allocation. Its purpose is to identify and bring to the planners' and policy makers' attention potential problem areas that could impact on the continuing viability and/or implementation of the development plan. These may relate to unanticipated conditions or outcomes in plan implementation, or to changes in environmental conditions that necessitate modifications in the direction, assumptions, strategies, or programs of the plan.

Technically, a strategic plan monitoring system has two broad dimensions. One dimension involves monitoring developments in selected areas of the plan. Operationally, this usually involves monitoring changes in the behaviour of selected key elements of the plan over time.[45] This part of the system comprises the traditional monitoring activity of tracking performance. It uses data about observed outcomes to focus attention on problem areas by identifying significant discrepancies between expected and actual outcomes.[46] This aspect of monitoring may be termed as *monitoring the past* in order to help make future adjustments.

Strategic monitoring in a turbulent environment must go beyond tracking past performance. A second dimension or requirement then involves the capability to use incomplete and uncertain information for drawing inferences about plan progress with respect to potential future outcomes. Operationally, this can take the form of tracing or inferring the possible implications or impacts of changes (actual or postulated) in one part of the plan or its environment, on other related parts. This can provide a kind of *early warning system* in anticipating potential problem areas by identifying possible future outcomes.

The *anticipatory* dimension of strategic monitoring should not be confused with forecasting in its various forms. Its role is not to predict future values of specific variables in a highly uncertain, dynamic and complex environment. It has the more modest objective of drawing attention to potential or possible outcomes that *may* result from known or postulated conditions. These possible outcomes, if judged both credible and significant, should then lead to more detailed and comprehensive analysis and discussion involving relevant interests. In technical terms, the inferences about potential future conditions or outcomes should not be construed as a forecast of the time behaviour of the system. Instead, they should be viewed as indicators of the stability characteristics of the structure of the plan in a changing environment.

The conceptual and technological basis for developing the elements of an *anticipatory monitoring system* at the macro planning level is now becoming available. It lies in developments relating to areas such as structural modelling, programmable relational databases and artificial intelligence.[47] However, there is very limited experience to date with this approach to plan management in either the public or private sector. The appropriate institutional environment for this approach to plan management is similarly unclear.[48]

Preliminary efforts are now under way in Thailand to improve the management of plan implementation. At the macro level, this includes early developments to support strategic monitoring capability at both the plan and program level. At the micro level, the new requirement to have implementing agencies develop annual operational plans for their particular areas of responsibility in program implementation can also be viewed as indirectly supporting the role of strategic monitoring. In principle, it implies a need for more detailed monitoring by implementing agencies of their activities, (including development projects implementing programs), as a basis for adjusting their annual operational plans. In this way, strategic and operational information needs in plan implementation are separated, reinforcing both the macro guidance role of central institutions and the operations management role of implementing agencies.

It is important to stress that these developments are in their early stages. Further work is needed in the conceptual, technical, institutional and administrative dimensions before they can contribute in any significant way to the development planning process. Ultimately, some level of experience in the implementation of these efforts is necessary before any, even preliminary observations can be made about their likely roles and contributions.

Conclusion

The process of development in Thailand has generally been judged successful by both absolute and relative standards. It has been characterized by both growth and structural change. The planning system has played a significant and evolving role in this transformation process.[49]

In approaching the formulation of the Seventh National Economic and Social Development Plan, the increasing diversity, complexity and urgency of development issues - both externally induced and domestically generated - are likely to put increasing pressures on the planning system. Important issues remain to a varying extent unresolved, as new issues emerge. Unresolved issues include the continuing problems of poverty and inequalities within the context of an increasingly complex socio-economic system. New issues include the pressure to diversify the product/market base of the economy for employment and income generation, in an increasingly competitive external environment, and in a domestic environment conditioned by growing constraints on the natural resource base. More generally, development planners in Thailand need to balance the requirements of international competitiveness as the basis for growth in an open economy, with the pressures for maintaining socio-economic stability and balance in an increasingly turbulent environment.

A central dilemma facing the planning system relates to the alternative approaches to development planning reflected in the optimizing/centralized approach that was so effective in earlier plans, and the interactive/decentralized approach that first emerged during the Fourth Plan. Both approaches were accommodated in the two programs of the Fifth Plan, and continue to be reflected in various guises in the Sixth Plan. The changing planning context, however, may sharpen both the differences in the two approaches, and their implications of these differences for the development planning system. This is especially relevant in the context of a changing political environment and its implications for economic decision making.

A full discussion of this issue would require a separate paper. We can note, however, that the two approaches provide potentially different and important choices with respect to key dimensions of the planning system - its orientation, supporting institutional arrangements, mechanisms and technology - in adjusting to changing conditions and requirements. They embody very different assumptions about the availability of information about conditions and preferences; about the nature and distribution of power and control in development; about the stability and predictability of outcomes and preferences; about the relationship between planning and implementation, and so on. The implications of these two different approaches for the planning system are yet to be fully explored, and the choices implied may have a significant impact on the nature of development in Thailand.

Notes

1. W.C. Baum and S.M. Tolbert, *Investing in Development* (Oxford: Oxford University Press, 1985), 19.

2. It is not our intention to measure the performance of development planning in Thailand. On this, see G. Paquet, "The Structuration of a Planned Economy", in *The Canadian Slavonic Papers*, (8, 1966), 251. We need simply establish the relationship between the changing focus and process of planning and development in order to assess its dynamic *fit*.

3. F. Perroux, *A New Concept of Development* (Paris: Croom Helm, 1983), 26.

4. Clearly this does not mean that growth is constant or permanent, or that decline and fluctuations are not possible. It means instead that growth occurs in irreversible time or history.

5. G. Abonyi, "Technology and Development: A Review and Overview", in *Planning for Technological Development Policy*, eds. R.A. Goodman and J. Pavon, (New York: Praeger, 1984), 49.

6. The term "stakeholder" is now generally accepted in the strategic management field. It refers to "any group, organization or institution which potentially has a vested interest, either direct or indirect" in a given problem. See G. Abonyi, "SIAM: Strategic Impact and Assumptions-Identification Method for Project, Program and Policy Planning", in *Technological Forecasting and Social Change*, (September 1982), 41.

7. J. Kornai, *Anti-Equilibrium* (Amsterdam: American Elsevier, 1971), 39.

8. This is not to imply that development management can be reduced to the *control* of selected quantitative indicators. However, for development management to be effective, it must

judge whether a problem exists, if it is worsening or if it is improving. This implies that changes in state can be *measured* through some form of qualitative or quantitative indicators, such as health care, education and employment.

9. The degree of openness of an economy is itself partly a function of development management decisions. That is, policies can aim at increasing or decreasing the domestic integration with the international economic system through various measures that support or hinder export/import orientation, investment flows, and so on.

10. Planning problems relate to needs or opportunities not met, unresolved issues, or more generally, unrealized values.

11. The term *norms* is used here to refer to desired ends in various forms, such as goals, objectives, targets and expected outcomes.

12. The term *feasible* is used in the conventional sense, meaning consistent with existing resources.

13. An example of the difference in the Thai context is referred to in chapter 4, contrasting infrastructure planning problems which tend to be well-structured, with the ill-structured problems of rural poverty alleviation and international competitiveness. For a more detailed discussion of the nature of ill-structured and wicked problems, see A.G. Gorry and M.S. Morton, "Management decisions systems: A framework for management information systems" in *Working Paper 458-470* (Cambridge: Alfred P. Sloan School of Management, 1970). See also H.W Rittel and M. Webber, "Dilemmas in the general theory of planning", in *Policy Sciences* 4, 2 (1973).

14. Adapted from P. Lassere, "Planning through incrementalism," *Socio-Economic Planning Sciences* 8 (3), 1974 and J.D. Thompson and A. Tuden, "Strategies, structures and processes of organization decision," in *Comparative Studies in Administration*, J.D. Thompson, P.B. Hammond, R.W. Hawkes, B.H. Junker and A. Tuden (eds.), (Pittsburgh: University of Pittsburgh Press, 1958).

15. Identifying and managing the different types of uncertainties in the planning problem require different methods and processes in the planning system. For an excellent discussion of this issue, see J.K. Friend and W.N. Jessop, *Local Government and Strategic Choice,* Part 2 (London: Tavistock Publications Ltd, 1969). See also, G. Vickers, *The Art of Judgement* (London: Methuen, 1965).

16. F.E. Emery, and E.L. Trist, "The Causal Texture of Organizational Environments" in *Human Relations,* 18 (1965), 26.

17. For a detailed development of the optimizing/centralized and interactive/decentralized approaches to planning see G. Abonyi, and B. Ninsananda, "Democratic Politics and Development Planning", in progress. See also, G. Abonyi, "Technique, Experts and Planning", in *University of Ottawa Quarterly*, 56 (December, 1986).

18. World Bank, East Asia Country Programs Department, *Thailand: Country Economic Report*, 1986, 6036-TH, 10.

19. "Thailand: Credit Overview", in (Solomon Brothers Inc., 1986).

20. Royal Thai Government, National Economic and Social Development Board, *National Economic and Social Development Plan 1961-1966,* Bangkok. Further references to the National Economic and Social Development Board are cited using the following abbreviation: NESDB.

21. Ibid.

22. NESDB, *National Income of Thailand: New Series 1970-1987.*

23. World Bank, East Asia Country Programs Department, *Income Growth and Poverty Alleviation in Thailand,* August 1980.

24. See "Adapting to Changing Conditions: The Fifth and Sixth Plans", and "Constrained Flexibility: Plans to Projects", for a discussion of the program-based approach, further in this text.

25. NESDB, *National Income of Thailand: New Series 1970-1987.*

26. Ibid.

27. World Bank, East Asia Country Programs Department, *Thailand: Country Economic Report*, 1986, 6036-TH, 3 (26).

28. World Bank, East Asia Country Programs Department, *Thailand: Managing Public Resources for Structural Adjustment,* 1-3. World Bank, Country Program Department, East Asia and Pacific Regional Office, August 31, 1983, 4366-TH, especially Part I. See also, *Thailand: Coping with Structural Change in a Dynamic Economy,* East Asia and Pacific Regional Office, December 23, 1980, 3067a-TH, especially Part II.

29. *Thailand: Managing Public Resources for Structural Adjustment.*

30. The Rural Poverty Alleviation Program was the first comprehensive and integrated effort aimed specifically at the rural poverty issue, utilizing an area-focused approach. Specific villages with the highest poverty levels were designated as targets, with particular strategies developed for addressing their needs based on the local and differentiated resource endowments. A multi-departmental management system was set up to implement this programme; relevant central and implementing agencies administered all stages of development programming for rural poverty alleviation from policy planning through monitoring and evaluation phases. From the perspective of the planning process, this programme attempted to create conditions for greater decentralization from central government to both local (rural) areas and implementing agencies, increasing participation in both project initiation and selection. In practice, villagers participated in the planning process by selecting from a prearranged menu of project options designed for each community by technical experts and based on local conditions. A key criterion for selection involved suitability to local conditions as perceived in part by the affected population. The second programme, the Eastern Seaboard Development Programme, was intended to simultaneously implement a strategy of basic industry development and geographic decentralization from the Bangkok area. It involved an ambitious and extensive investment program designed to extend Thailand's basic industry development. This program was built around the discovery of natural gas in the Gulf of Thailand and on the

geographical conditions of the Eastern Seaboard region as a transportation centre. It was to include the construction of two major sea ports and related infrastructure, as well as the promotion of various basic industries, such as petrochemicals, designed to utilize the port facilities. The programme was implemented by a unit established as part of the central planning agency with the optimization of public investment as a key criterion for choice.

31. World Bank, East Asia Country Programs Department, *Thailand: Country Economic Report*, 1986, Part V.

32. Ibid, Part I.

33. See for example, *Thailand: Country Economic Report, Part II*, 156.

34. NESDB, 1981-1986.

35. D. Schon, *Beyond the Stable State*, (New York: W. Norton and Co., 1973). See especially Chapter 1.

36. A turbulent environment is also likely to be a reasonably good proxy for the existence of ill-structured planning problems, given the earlier discussion of the planning context. This describes the Thai environment, as a comparison of the planning context in Plans 1 and 2 with Plans 4, 5 and 6 can demonstrate.

37. *Thailand: Country Economic Report*, 14.

38. G. Abonyi, "SIAM: Strategic Impact and Assumptions-Identification Method for Project, Program and Policy Planning", in *Technological Forecasting and Social Change*, (September 1982), 34.

39. This paragraph draws on P. Wack, "Scenarios: shooting the rapids", in *Harvard Business Review*, (November-December 1985).

40. For example, it is difficult to project what the future international competitive environment will look like. However, it is possible to build alternative scenarios incorporating different assumptions about the nature and extent

of protectionism in key markets. Proposed production and export strategies can then be tested against these scenarios.

41. See for example R.L. Ackoff, *Creating the Corporate Future* (New York: John Wiley and Sons, 1981). See also, "Scenarios: shooting the rapids".

42. *Sixth National Economic and Social Development Plan* (1981-1986).

43. S. Beer, "The Aborting Corporate Plan - A Cybernetic Account of the Interface between Planning and Action", in *Perspectives of Planning*, Organization for Economic Cooperation and Development, (1968) 397.

44. Ibid, 398.

45. Changes in the status of plan elements are monitored via changes in the values of associated indicators. For a detailed development of a framework for strategic plan monitoring, including a discussion of the nature and role of indicators, see G. Abonyi, "A Framework for Strategic Control", forthcoming.

46. For a well known example of such a system, see Government of Malaysia-UNDP-World Bank, State and Rural Development Project, *Guidelines for Monitoring and Evaluation,* 1981.

47. For a discussion of these issues, see "A Framework for Strategic Control". See also, S. Beer, *Brain of the Firm* (New York: John Wiley and Sons, 1981). Finally, see P. Lorange et. al., *Strategic Control* (St. Paul: West Publishing Co., 1986).

48. For an attempt to derive the required institutional framework, see *Brain of the Firm.*

49. It is useful to place discussions of the Thai planning system in an institutional context. As noted, the agency responsible for managing the development planning process is the NESDB. It is nominally attached to the Office of the Prime Minister and is headed by a Secretary General who also serves as the Secretary to the Council of Economic Ministers. The Secretary General is responsible to the Board of NESDB whose main function is to approve drafts of the national development plan. The plan itself is primarily the work of the staff of NESDB,

in consultation with other government agencies and external stakeholders. The process of plan formulation (e.g. in the Sixth Plan) begins with the overall macro framework of plan preparation by senior NESDB staff, in consultation with other agencies. This becomes the basis for more detailed development involving a number of ad hoc working groups with a wide representation of interests. Draft reports are discussed with appropriate implementing agencies. The final draft plan is submitted to the NESDB Management Committee and to the Board, followed by the Council of Economic Ministers for review and approval. Once approved by Cabinet, it is signed into law by His Majesty the King.

There is no official role in the plan formulation process for other central agencies, although there is close and continuous informal consultation. In the implementation of the plan, however, the Ministry of Finance (in particular the Fiscal Policy Office) and the Bureau of the Budget play, an important role. They play a particularly key role in the project review and selection process that transforms the broad framework of the plan into a public investment program.

References

Abonyi, G., "Technique, Experts and Planning", B. Bazoge and G. Paquet, *University of Ottawa Quarterly*, 56 (4), December, 1986.

Abonyi, G. and N. Howard, "A Boolean Approach to Interactive Program Planning", *Management Science*, 26 (7), July, 1980.

Abonyi, G., "A Framework for Strategic Control," (forthcoming).

Beer, S., *Brain of the Firm*, 2nd ed., New York: John Wiley and Sons, 1981.

Beer, S., *The Heart of Enterprise*, New York: John Wiley and Sons, 1979.

Friedmann, J., *Retracking America: A Theory of Transactive Planning*, New York: Anchor Press, 1973.

Friedmann, J. and G. Abonyi, "Social learning: a model for policy research", *Environment and Planning A*, 8, 1976.

Friend, J.K. and W.N. Jessop, *Local Government and Strategic Choice*, London: Tavistock Publications Ltd., 1969.

Frisch, R., "Economic Planning and the Growth Problem in Developing Countries", Oslo: University of Oslo, Institute of Economics, 1961.

Government of Malaysia, *Guidelines for Monitoring and Evaluation*, Government of Malaysia - UNDP/World Bank, State and Rural Development Project, July, 1981.

Lassere, P., "Planning through incrementalism", *Socio-Economic Planning Sciences* 8 (3), 1974.

Lorange, P., M. F. Scott Morton and S. Ghoshal, *Strategic Control*, St. Paul: West Publishing Co., 1986.

Paquet, G., "The Structuration of a Planned Economy", *Canadian Slavonic Papers*, 8, 1966.

Polanyi, K., *The Great Transformation*, Boston: Beacon Press, 1944.

Rittel, H.W. and M. Webber, "Dilemmas in the general theory of planning", *Policy Sciences*, 4 (2), 1973.

Snoh Unakul, "Annual Planning in Thailand," *Economic Bulletin for Asia and the Far East*, 1 (20), 1969.

Thompson, J.D. and A. Tuden, "Strategies, structures and processes of organization decision", in *Comparative Studies in Administration*, J.D. Thompson, P.B. Hammond, R.W. Hawkes, B.H. Junker and A. Tuden (eds.), Pittsburgh: University of Pittsburgh Press, 1958.

Twatchai Yongkittikul, "The Thai Economy in the 1980s: Significant Issues, Problems and Prospects", in Somsakdi Xuto, Suchart Prasithrathsint, Thinapan Nakata, and Twatchai Yongkittikul, *Thailand in the 1980s: Significant Issues, Problems and Prospects*, Bangkok: TURA Institute, 1981.

Twatchai Yongkittikul and Chaiyawat Wibulswasdi, "Strategies and Measures for Thailand's Economic Development in the 1980s" in Somsakdi Xuto, Suchart Prasithrathsint, Thinapan Nakata, Twatchai Yongkittikul, *Strategies and Measures for the Development of Thailand in the 1980s*, Bangkok: TURA Institute, 1983.

Vanston, J.H., W.P. Frisbie, S.C. Lopreato, and D.L. Poston, "Alternate Scenario Planning", *Technological Forecasting and Social Change*, 10, 1977.

Vickers, G., *The Art of Judgment*, London: Methuen, University Paperbacks, 1965.

Wack, P., "Scenarios: Uncharted Waters Ahead", *Harvard Business Review*, September-October, 1985.

World Bank, *Thailand: Toward a Development Strategy of Full Participation*, The World Bank, 1980.

World Bank, *Institutional Aspects of Development in Thailand*, Working Paper, East Asia and Pacific Programs Department, 1978.

About the Authors

George Abonyi is an Associate Professor of Strategic Management at the Faculty of Administration, University of Ottawa. He is on special leave as advisor to the National Economic and Social Development Board (NESDB), Royal Thai Government, where he also served as an advisor from 1983-85. The NESDB is the central planning agency of the Royal Thai Government and is responsible for the management of the development planning process. Dr. Abonyi received his Ph.D. from the University of California at Los Angeles, and has written, lectured and consulted in Canada and abroad in the areas of strategic analysis, development planning and competitive industry analysis.

Bunyaraks Ninsananda is the Director of the Overall Planning Division of the National Economic and Social Development Board. Within the NESDB, Dr. Bunyarak's present responsibilities include macro planning and policy support activities related to development planning and management. Dr. Bunyaraks received his Ph.D. from the Fletcher School of Law and Diplomacy, Tufts University, Medford, Massachussetts. He has written and lectured on development planning and economic managment in Thailand and abroad.

Asia Papers

Joint Centre for Asia Pacific Studies

Richard Stubbs, comp. *Vietnam: Facing the 1990s.* Asia Papers No. 1 1989.

Mitchell Bernard. *Northeast Asia: The Political Economy of a Post-war Regional System.* Asia Papers No. 2 1989.

George Abonyi and Bunyaraks Ninsananda. *Thailand: Development Planning in Turbulent Times.* Asia Papers No. 3 1989.

Forthcoming:

Diana Lary. *Dumb Foreigners: Language and Cultural Barriers to Canadian Relations with Asia and the Pacific.* Revised Edition. Asia Papers No. 4 1989.

The Joint Centre for Asia Pacific Studies' objectives are: to promote scholarly research on the Asia Pacific Region and Canadian involvement with it; to foster exchanges with Asian institutions; to encourage cooperation among academic specialists in modern Asian studies; to facilitate improved interchange with government and business; and to promote public understanding.

The Joint Centre, established in 1974, is a university-based, non-profit organization with support from private and public organizations in Ontario and elsewhere.